T0107324

THE MASSACHUSETTS TECHNOLOGY DEVELOPMENT CORPORATION (MTDC)

How the Massachusetts Venture Capital Firm
Leveraged Private Investments to Create Jobs

John F. Hodgman

THE MASSACHUSETTS TECHNOLOGY DEVELOPMENT CORPORATION (MTDC)
HOW THE MASSACHUSETTS VENTURE CAPITAL FIRM LEVERAGED PRIVATE INVESTMENTS TO CREATE JOBS

iUniverse books may be ordered through booksellers or by contacting:

iUniverse
1663 Liberty Drive
Bloomington, IN 47403
www.iuniverse.com
1-800-Authors (1-800-288-4677)

ISBN: 978-1-4917-5996-7 (sc)
ISBN: 978-1-4917-5995-0 (e)

Library of Congress Control Number: 2015901923

Print information available on the last page.

iUniverse rev. date: 05/11/2015

CONTENTS

AUTHOR'S NOTE

As president of the Massachusetts Technology Development Corporation (MTDC) between 1984 and 2001, I had the opportunity and privilege to lead a unique public-private partnership designed to leverage private capital with a small amount of public dollars to help launch and grow almost 140 start-up and early-stage technology companies in Massachusetts. This venture capital firm was started by the Commonwealth of Massachusetts in 1978 and continues today, operating since 2012 as MassVentures.

The Massachusetts economy was in bad shape in the mid-1970s. The long-term loss of traditional manufacturing jobs to lower-cost states was exacerbated by the recession of 1973 to 1974. The national rate of inflation exceeded 10 percent during 1974 and early 1975. Consumer spending was down, and the Massachusetts unemployment rate increased to 12.3 percent. Finally, the decline in defense spending that had helped to fuel Massachusetts's high-tech economic engine had resulted in job cuts among technology firms.

Newly elected governor Michael Dukakis began his first term in January 1975 and was faced with the challenge of creating tens of thousands of new jobs. The lack of credit and venture capital for start-up and emerging technology companies led his administration to propose the creation of several state quasi-public organizations that would help to finance these young enterprises. The MTDC was one of these firms.

The book I have written tells the story of why and how the MTDC was created and traces its history over the last two decades of the twentieth century. While I have described the inner workings of this unique quasi-public corporation, I have also tried to depict the changing patterns of technology start-ups and private venture capital during these years. Many of the technology companies that the MTDC helped to finance were pioneers in the development of computer-based tools and systems that we take for granted today. I have also included several case studies in the book in which entrepreneurs the MTDC backed tell their stories.

When the MTDC was created in 1978, I was the director of the Massachusetts Employment Security Agency. At the time, a major concern of the leaders of the Commonwealth's minicomputer industry was the supply of hardware engineers. By the time I joined the MTDC in 1984, the minicomputer industry was beginning to be threatened by the growing use of desktop computers and software independent from hardware. Ultimately, the minicomputer manufacturing companies declined, and a new wave of technology-based enterprises began to grow. This experience taught me the critical importance to our economic welfare of nurturing new technology company start-ups.

As of the end of MassVentures's fiscal year on June 30, 2014, total capital for the investment fund came from the federal government ($2,972,000) and the Commonwealth ($12,700,000). Between 1978 and 2014, cumulative investments of these funds totaled $85.4 million and had helped 139 companies start and grow. For every one dollar invested by the corporation, four to five dollars of private coinvestment had initially been made in these companies. Total net realized gains were $28.7 million. Finally, between 1984 and 2014, the estimated average annual jobs among the companies the MTDC had backed totaled over 5,400.

My objective in writing this book is to document the history of the MTDC. When I retired from the corporation in 2001, I had accumulated seven file boxes of personal papers, which enabled me to reference original sources as I wrote the book.

Since retirement, I have taught entrepreneurship courses at Tufts University and have continued to observe the dynamics of the entrepreneurial and venture capital communities in the Boston area. While the size of venture funds has grown dramatically, technologies have evolved significantly, and both the entrepreneurs and investors have changed; the systems that create new companies employing thousands of men and women continue to maintain the innovation economy of the Commonwealth.

John F. Hodgman
January 2015

INTRODUCTION

In the winter and spring of 1974, if you didn't run out of gas waiting in long lines to buy more fuel for your car, you found the price per gallon had increased by over 40 percent from the previous year. President Nixon requested that gasoline stations not sell fuel on Saturday nights and Sundays. Gas lines during weekdays became a regular experience. This is how the average citizen felt the impact of the October 1973 OPEC oil embargo.

While the embargo was lifted in March 1974, the national economy was shocked into a recession as the price of energy continued to rise. In addition, the reductions in defense research spending that had boosted the Massachusetts high-tech sector made the Commonwealth especially vulnerable. It was a grim time for political leaders.

When Michael Dukakis became governor for the first time in January 1975, he found that unemployment in the Commonwealth had peaked at 12.3 percent. Over a long period, many Massachusetts manufacturing companies had fled to regions where labor and energy costs were lower. It was clear that reversing this trend would be a major challenge. The new governor appointed Howard Smith as his secretary of manpower affairs and assigned him the task of developing the Commonwealth's economic-development strategy.

Smith had a long career as a business executive, but this was his first job in public service. He welcomed the economic-development challenge and promptly printed stationery and business cards changing his title to secretary of economic affairs. This drew the ire of the then Speaker of the House of Representatives Thomas McGee, who reminded Smith that such title changes had to be enacted into law. When Smith explained that the title of secretary of economic affairs more accurately described his role, McGee told him that in the legislature "king of the hill" more accurately described his job but the constitution named him Speaker.

The exquisite challenge of designing and implementing a state economic-development strategy in a charged political environment is underscored by this story. Smith regrouped and began to learn how to maneuver in this setting. However, the poor economy left little room for the long delays required by the political process. Smith and his team had to move fast.

In the spring, a reporter asked Smith if Massachusetts could survive. In his usual blunt style, he responded, "Calcutta survives." The real question was what kind of economic future we desired for the Commonwealth.

Smith looked at the thousands of jobs that had been lost and tried to estimate how many could be created by trying to attract new employers from outside the state, versus new jobs from start-ups and the expansion of existing Massachusetts companies. He decided the homegrown strategy offered more potential and began to work with the governor's staff to develop a plan.

Among the first steps was a systematic survey of what emerging and established Massachusetts employers said they needed. At the top of the response list was reform of the unemployment insurance law, which had created a situation where employees could quit their jobs and then begin to collect benefits. This was very costly and demoralizing. The Dukakis administration worked with the legislature to revise the laws and started to reduce the cost of unemployment insurance.

Next on the response list was the difficulty that new and emerging companies were having in finding credit and investment dollars. During the 1974 recession, capital markets throughout the nation had become severely constrained. Promising new companies and mature firms seeking financing to rejuvenate were having great difficulty securing capital.

In order to address the problem, the governor's staff and Smith's team created a "Governor's Capital Formation Task Force." Its recommendations became part of the overall plan that was published in August 1976 entitled "An Economic Program for Massachusetts." On page 16 of that document was the following recommendation:

> Creation of a state new Enterprises Development Corporation which would help Massachusetts regain its competitive advantage in fostering the creation of *new*, high value added, high technology industries. With initial funding from the state, this professionally staffed Massachusetts corporation would join with other private venture capitalists to provide start up financing of new, technologically innovative businesses.[1]

This recommendation described the mission of what came to be called the Massachusetts Technology Development Corporation (MTDC).

The next step was to pass legislation to create four innovative financing organizations that focused on homegrown businesses.

The following were established in 1977 and 1978:

- the Massachusetts Capital Resource Corporation (MCRC)
- the Massachusetts Industrial Finance Agency (MIFA)
- the Massachusetts Community Development Finance Corporation (CDFC)

- the Massachusetts Technology Development Corporation (MTDC)

Frank Keefe was the governor's director of planning during this period and was instrumental in developing and helping to get the legislature to create these organizations. When I met Frank in January 2014, he recalled how the creation of MIFA, CDFC, and MTDC took place in the very last hours of the legislative session, and that the MTDC rode in on the coattails of the political momentum of the other two agencies.

While all of these financing organizations played major roles by leveraging private capital to help the state to revitalize its economy, this is the story of the MTDC, the Commonwealth's venture capital firm.

CHAPTER 1
BEGINNINGS

Pioneers and Precedents

In Massachusetts, the use of venture capital to create new enterprises is very old. In 1620, the "Separatists" (Pilgrims) and "Strangers" launched the enterprise that began in Plymouth, having been financed by a London venture capitalist, Thomas Weston.[2] However, let us focus on Massachusetts in the early twentieth century. Three hundred years later, business and political leaders trying to find ways to revitalize the economy formed the New England Council. The following excerpt from the council website describes how this organization came into being.[3]

> In the 1920s, the New England economy was at a crossroads. Warmer temperatures and cheaper costs were luring many of the region's companies south, and the textile and shoe manufacturers that had long anchored many communities were closing shop.
>
> In June 1925, a group of New England business leaders and the region's six governors gathered in Poland Spring, Maine, to develop a strategy to address these problems and promote economic growth. It was at this strategy session deep in the woods of Maine where this group of

> business and government leaders laid the groundwork for what would become the New England Council.
>
> The "New England Conference" followed up the Poland Springs meeting in November 1925 in Worcester, Massachusetts. Approximately 800 representatives of agricultural, industrial, and commercial organizations throughout New England attended the conference. After two days discussing the challenges facing the New England economy, the delegates made two decisions. First, they decided to make the New England Conference an annual event, and second, they created a permanent executive body, The New England Council, to give concrete expression to the ideas and purposes developed at the Conference.

This early partnership of private and public leaders began to work on a number of strategies. One of these was to create a pool of venture capital to help launch new technology-based enterprises that might arise from research and talent found at MIT, Harvard, and many of the area's other colleges and universities. Once the Great Depression began to stifle career opportunities for graduates of these institutions, it became more urgent to find ways to create new enterprises.

The second world war intervened when the United States joined the Allies in 1941. The military and industrial needs of the country required all the talent that was available in New England. However, a few wise men kept the concept of a venture capital pool on the shelf until peacetime resumed. In 1946, these leaders launched the American Research and Development Corporation (ARD).[4]

Ralph Flanders, an industrialist and later US senator from Vermont, and Carl Compton, president of MIT, were among the leaders who recruited Georges Doriot from the Harvard Business School to become the president of ARD. Doriot's business philosophy guided the development of this first institutional venture capital firm in the United States.

ARD sent its staff out to meet with scientists and engineers working in the labs of educational and government institutions to find inventions and innovations that had the potential to be commercialized. Among these were Ken Olsen and Harlan Anderson, who went on to become the founders of Digital Equipment Corporation (DEC). ARD became the first and major investor in this company. DEC went on to become the second-largest computer company after IBM in the early 1980s. Many of its former employees left to start hundreds of new technology companies that changed the landscape of the Massachusetts high-tech community.

ARD was a pioneer, along with a few family firms, in the development of the venture capital industry in the United States. In 1958, the US Congress passed the Small Business Investment Company Act, which spurred the growth of institutional venture capital organizations. Then in the 1960s, the establishment of private venture capital partnerships created the model that continues to be the predominant legal structure for venture capital investing.

Swords into Ploughshares

Beginning with World War II and continuing into the Cold War, the defense budget of the United States allocated billions of dollars to fund research into the use of science and technology for military purposes. Large amounts of these dollars went to universities like MIT and built up a robust pool of research talent. This phenomenon was accelerated after the 1957 launch of Sputnik by the Soviet Union stimulated a technological arms race. The National Defense Education Act in 1958 significantly increased the funding to develop scientific and technological talent in the United States.

This abundance of research could yield solutions to problems in civilian life. There were efforts to commercialize many of the inventions and innovations developed through government-funded research. While it would not be until the 1980s when the Bayh-Dole Act formalized the necessary legal structures, a few far-thinking Massachusetts leaders, including the former president of MIT Jerome Wiesner, advocated that Massachusetts take steps to commercialize government-funded research.

In 1969, these leaders persuaded the legislature and governor of the Commonwealth to create the Massachusetts Science and Technology Foundation (MSTF). The enabling act provided that:

> The purposes of the Foundation shall be to encourage, promote and assist basic and applied scientific and technological research and development in the Commonwealth; and to establish therein facilities for said purposes.[5]

One of the programs operated by the MSTF was a service to advise technology-oriented entrepreneurs about how to secure funding to launch their new enterprises. Often these entrepreneurs were experiencing difficulty raising capital. They were developing innovative products for markets that had yet to mature. In addition, they were seeking relatively small amounts of funding.

The MSTF management-assistance program helped these entrepreneurs develop business plans and access sources of capital. The public policy of encouraging scientists, engineers, and technologists to bring their inventions and innovations to use through entrepreneurial companies was now being recognized as a critical resource for the economic revitalization of Massachusetts and the United States.

Flattery by Imitation

When the Dukakis Capital Formation Task Force looked for models for the MTDC, ARD, SBIC, and venture capital partnerships were readily available. The mission and history of the MSTF influenced the specific focus on early-stage technology companies. In particular, the chronic "capital gap" encountered by early-stage technology-based entrepreneurs underscored the need for an unusual type of venture capital firm.

In fact in 1975, the MSTF proposed the establishment of a Massachusetts Technology Development Corporation and filed a bill (House 5937) that would have created such an entity. In August 1975, the president of the MSTF, Dr. John Silvers, had prepared a "Proposal for Funding Support to Establish the Massachusetts Technology Development Corporation," assisted by Lee Steele, who thirty years later would become a member of the board of directors of the MTDC. In addition, Paul Kelley, who worked at the MSTF and would later leave the MTDC to form Zero Stage Capital, played an important role in developing the framework for the corporation's investment program.

The proposal called for $3.5 million from the Commonwealth to fund a program that would provide "capital stimulation incentives … required to make private resources, both managerial and financial, more effective in the process of technology commercialization." The fund would have the option of providing guarantees to any one project of up to $300,000 of a portion of private investments or direct financial assistance of up to $150,000. Returns to the MTDC would be in the form of royalties on sales of products and fees. It was anticipated that revenues from these sources would enable the program to become self-sufficient and repay public monies. The plan projected that at the end of ten years, twenty-two new firms would be created, employing 1,100 in direct new jobs.[6]

The drafters of the legislation creating MTDC looked at the MSTF charter and experiences and decided to have the new entity take over the assets and liabilities of the MSTF. The historic collaboration among higher education, government, and business that were part of MSTF's modus operandi became part of the culture of the MTDC. In addition, the MSTF management-assistance program was carried over directly to the MTDC.

The MTDC investment program had to be developed from scratch. The existing models of ARD and the SBIC program were to become useful templates.

Turning Concepts into Laws

As mentioned earlier, the recommendation to create the MTDC was one of several made by the governor's Capital Formation Task Force. The concept of the enterprise was that it would be a quasi-public corporation with an indefinite life. It would be governed by a board of directors comprised of eight private-sector individuals and three ex officio state government officials. Its mission and operating policies would be specified in its enabling statute so that it would focus exclusively on seed and early-stage technology companies based in Massachusetts. Its fundamental goal was to increase employment in Massachusetts through the creation and growth of these companies. Finally, the plan called for the corporation to be capitalized with $10 million for its investment fund and operations.

When the MTDC enabling act was passed in 1978, the governance structure, mission, policies, and purposes were all included. However, there was no appropriation for the investment program. The story commonly reported was that some members of the local venture capital community were not eager to see the Commonwealth become a potential competitor, perhaps offering more favorable terms to entrepreneurs. In addition, there was and continues to be a concern about government programs that "pick winners and losers." What some of these venture capitalists did not realize was that the legal requirements of the MTDC mandated that it collaborate in leveraging private coinvestments in companies on equal terms. As a result, over the years many of the local venture capital firms participated in deals with the MTDC. Nevertheless, there was a successful lobbying effort to stop any appropriations for the MTDC investment program.

At this point the MTDC might have been considered "stillborn." Instead, there was an operating budget appropriation to continue the staff of what was previously the MSTF. This operating appropriation was conditioned as an advance to ultimately be repaid to the Commonwealth, along with the cumulative appropriations since 1969 for the MSTF. This liability that was transferred from MSTF to the new MTDC was about $1.2 million.

Entrepreneurial Creativity

In September 1978, an unexpected outcome of the Democratic primary was that the incumbent governor, Michael Dukakis, lost his party's nomination to Edward King. This political change interrupted the plans for the development of the MTDC, which had been created by Governor Dukakis. However, there was some continuity of leadership between the two administrations.

The lieutenant governor under Michael Dukakis was Thomas O'Neill Jr. Lt. Governor O'Neill was nominated by the Democratic Party to continue under Edward King. When the King-O'Neill team took office in 1979, Lt. Governor O'Neill was one of the three ex officio members of the MTDC board of directors.

While the cabinet-level officials in the Dukakis administration were replaced, the King administration held over a number of the key people at the next levels of government. One of these was William Aikman, general counsel in the executive office of manpower affairs (subsequently economic affairs). Aikman's task was to carry forward the launch of the several quasi-public financing agencies that had been created in 1978.

With the assistance of Lt. Governor O'Neill, Aikman and the board of directors of the MTDC developed a strategy to secure investment funds for the corporation. They approached the Economic Development Administration (EDA) of the US Department of Commerce for a revolving loan fund grant. The Speaker of the US House of Representatives at the time, Thomas O'Neill—father of the lieutenant governor—was especially helpful in securing an initial grant of $2 million to establish a revolving loan fund.

In the last year of President Carter's administration, a White House initiative called the Corporations for Innovation Development (CID) was established, and the EDA was charged with administration of this program. The MTDC secured a second grant for $1 million for a CID loan fund, to be matched by $1 million for an equity investment fund from the Commonwealth of Massachusetts. Although this federal grant was awarded to the MTDC, the incoming administration of President Reagan did not want to follow through with the distribution of funds. However, the MTDC's case ultimately prevailed. With the $1 million federal grant in hand, the MTDC persuaded the administration of Governor King and the legislature to agree to appropriate $1 million for the matching equity fund.

Investment Funds in Place

Now that the MTDC had $4 million, its investment program was able to commence. The challenge was how to identify the appropriate types of companies that met the requirements of the funding sources. By its charter, the MTDC needed to find that a company was having difficulty raising capital on affordable terms before it could invest. It also had to find that acceptable coinvestors would be willing to join in each investment syndicate. The $2 million EDA revolving loan fund and the $1 million federal CID loan fund were restricted to debt investments, and only the $1 million Massachusetts CID fund could be used for stock purchases.

Since the EDA loan fund was the first pool of capital available, the MTDC decided to focus on established technology companies that were bringing new products to market and would be able to service debt. These companies were generally seeking investments that were too small for venture capital partnerships. By starting with these types of companies, MTDC's staff was able to gain experience while making less-risky investments. On the other hand, because of the potential risk of loss, these companies agreed to not only pay a higher rate of interest on the loans but also provide an equity feature, such as a warrant to purchase stock at a future date.

The CID funds were targeted at start-up companies. Since these firms could not support the debt service, the investments were creatively structured. For example, if a company needed $200,000 from the MTDC, $150,000 might be in the form of a five-year convertible note and $50,000 might be in the form of the purchase of preferred convertible shares. The note might require payment of only interest during the first two years and then principal payments for the remaining three. This approach enabled start-up companies to begin operations without a heavy cash drain in their initial years of operations. In addition, by the time principal repayments were to begin, the MTDC might elect to convert the note into shares of the company. These types of investments were nicknamed "debtquity."

Investment Criteria

Because the charter of the MTDC limited investments to early-stage technology-based companies, the board and staff focused on and developed expertise with these types of enterprises. Engineers, scientists, and technology company managers who had not previously started businesses would become the principal sources of new enterprises. The temptation to stray into business sectors that were beyond the team's core competencies was avoided.

Before an investment could be approved, the company had to demonstrate that it was having difficulty raising capital. This turned out to be quite helpful in establishing an initial valuation of each deal. These valuations tended to be appropriately priced in relationship to the high degree of risk associated with start-ups.

The requirement to attract private coinvestors helped to bring independent perspectives to each deal. This also helped to avoid both the reality and the perception that investment decisions could be influenced by political considerations.

The practices were reinforced by the legal requirements of the MTDC. It was created as an economic development organization of the Commonwealth of Massachusetts, so its charter spelled out specific investment criteria and limitations. The authority for its operations and investments was delegated to its board of directors, who would hire and supervise its staff. The board was charged with making key findings before any investment by MTDC could be approved.

The MTDC Enabling Act, Chapter 497, Acts of 1978, amending Chapter 40G of the Massachusetts General Laws (MGL), spelled out the key investment criteria as follows:

The board shall find … that:

1. the proceeds of the investment will be used to cover the seed capital needs of the enterprise;
2. the enterprise has a reasonable chance of success;
3. the MTDC participation is necessary to the success of the enterprise because funding for the enterprise is unavailable in the traditional capital markets, or because funding has been offered on terms that would substantially hinder the success of the enterprise;
4. the enterprise has the reasonable potential to create a substantial amount of primary employment within the commonwealth and this employment, so far as feasible, may be expected to be for residents of target areas as defined in chapter forty F (MGL); and offers employment opportunities to unskilled and semiskilled individuals;
5. the entrepreneur and other founders of the enterprise have already made or are prepared to make a substantial financial and time commitment to the enterprise;
6. the securities purchased are qualified securities;
7. there is a reasonable possibility that the MTDC will recoup at least its initial investment; and
8. binding commitments have been made to the MTDC by the enterprise for adequate reporting of financial data to the MTDC, which shall include a requirement for an annual or other periodic audit of the books of the enterprise, and for such control on the part of the MTDC as the board shall consider prudent over the management of the enterprise, so as to protect the investment of the MTDC, including, in the discretion of the board and without limitation, right of access to financial and other records of the enterprise.

   If the MTDC makes a direct investment, the board shall also find that:
9. a reasonable effort has been made to find a professional investor to make an investment in the enterprise as a co-venture, and

> that such effort was unsuccessful. Such findings by the board shall be conclusive.

In addition, the MTDC was limited to making up to a $500,000 investment in any one enterprise, unless needed to protect an earlier investment, when the total could go to $1 million. MTDC was also limited to owning no more than 49 percent of the voting stock of an enterprise, "except that in the event of severe financial difficulty of the enterprise, threatening, in the judgment of the board, the investment of the MTDC therein, a greater percentage of such securities may be owned by the MTDC."[7]

These investment criteria and limitations were very different from those found in private venture capital partnerships. The key investment goal of a private venture capital firm is to achieve a very high rate of financial return. Job creation is a by-product, not a primary objective. On the other hand, sharing the cost of due diligence and the management of the risks associated with start-ups attracted private coinvestors to partner with the MTDC. MTDC became viewed as a very professional and reliable coinvestor.

The MTDC investment criteria did not require the corporation to seek high returns on its investments commensurate with the risk profile of the enterprises it was charged to finance. This presented a challenging paradox. However, the requirement to have private coinvestors drove the MTDC to participate in deals that would result in high rates of return.

In addition, there would be substantial tax benefits from being a public instrumentality of the Commonwealth of Massachusetts. All of MTDC's income and net capital gains from investments were tax-exempt at both the federal and state levels. In addition, its average cost per professional was substantially less than for a private VC firm because the salary levels and incentive compensation were limited by the standards for public employees. These economic advantages made it more likely that the MTDC could continue to focus on smaller investment transactions with very early-stage companies and be very patient about the timing of its harvests.

A June 1979 *Boston Globe* op-ed piece by David Warsh reported that: "The kind of company MTDC is looking for is the sort that falls in between the cracks at the larger modern venture capital businesses that are in Boston, and that has outgrown the resources that families and friends can provide, and that hasn't been able to tap the speculative 'doctor money' that abounds in Boston ..."[8]

Investment Program Launched

MTDC's first investment of $250,000 was made in December 1979 in Spire Corporation in the form of a debt instrument with warrants. In 1980, a total of $850,000 was invested among five companies: Discom, Xylogics, Solenergy, Saum, and Icon. Spire and Solenergy developed alternative energy products and systems. Discom and Xylogics produced computer hardware components. Icon developed factory automation systems, and Saum produced a plastics molding technology. These six initial investments were the beta tests of the investment process.

The MTDC investment process included the following steps:

1. The staff member responsible for a prospective investment would undertake "due diligence" on a case he or she was preparing to recommend to the investment committee of the board. This resulted in a thirty- to forty-page investment report for each company. (These reports came to be called "blue books" because of the color of the covers in which they were bound.)
2. A member, or members, of the investment committee would visit the company with the staff.
3. The principals of the company would meet with the investment committee members, who had previously received the "blue

book." After a rigorous examination of the case, the investment committee would recommend an investment in the company to the full board of directors for approval.

4. If six of the eleven members of the MTDC board voted in favor, the investment was approved.
5. The MTDC staff would then execute the closing documents and begin to follow the new company in its portfolio.

This process proved to be effective and has been followed substantially for the past thirty-five years.

MTDC's Entrepreneurs

In 2012 Robert Frohman worked with me to complete his individual leadership project report for his MS in engineering management at the Tufts Gordon Institute. His ILP was finished in August 2012 and was titled "Technology Entrepreneurship: Analyses from the MTDC Portfolio." Rob interviewed several MTDC entrepreneurs to whom I provided introductions. He described these individuals as follows:

> Technology leaders can be viewed as falling into three categories. There are the organization builders or technical leaders who are adept at building large organizations. Jack Welsh seems to fit this profile, starting his career at GE as a chemical engineer and moving up through the ranks to eventually become GE's youngest CEO. Next come the innovators with personalities like Steve Jobs and Thomas Edison as examples. These creative and innovative people are unstoppable in their pursuit of invention and equally as adamant that their inventions take root in the marketplace. The latter characteristic is the differentiator between an inventor and an innovator. Third are the

> enterprise creators which is the focus of this paper as these technology leaders demonstrate at their center an entrepreneurial spirit which, if provided the chance and resources, are the ones who can significantly drive economic development through business and job creation.[9]

Among the entrepreneurs the MTDC backed in the first phase of its investment program was Wayne Griffith. Wayne's story is recounted below from an interview with Rob Frohman.

Wayne Griffith—Xylogics and College Counsel

Wayne Griffith started his career with AT&T (NYSE) in their Executive Management Program. Following some time there, in order to earn more money, he joined AMP Inc. (NYSE) in Sales. Through several moves and promotions, and while working at AMP as District Sales Mgr./Midwest, based in Chicago, Mr. Griffith earned an M.B.A. in Marketing from Northwestern University. During his 12 years at AMP Inc., Mr. Griffith advanced from sales engineer to VP of all International Sales and Marketing, which was ½ of AMP's total business, approaching $1 Billion.

Mr. Griffith was hired away from AMP Inc. by Burndy Corp. (NYSE) to become Group VP of all international operations with responsibility for: mfg., engineering, development, finance, sales, marketing, distribution, etc. with plants in 10 countries. At Burndy he did a turnaround of all international operations increasing profitability from 20% of total corporate earnings to 60% in just 4 years. Mr. Griffith was then hired to become Executive Vice President of Leeds & Northrup - General Signal to focus on their international operations where he turned a losing business into a profitable one in less than 12 months. Mr. Griffith's background spanned over 18 years, traveling over 75% of the time and eventually overseeing >8000 people. In 1978 in order to reduce the demanding travel and address a growing family situation, Mr. Griffith decided to leave the large corporate world and do a "start-up" of his own.

An opportunity presented itself and Mr. Griffith moved into entrepreneurship as CEO of a 9 person company, Xylogics in Burlington, MA. Having been very successful managing large corporations, the transition to running a very small one proved to be interesting. Although having experience dealing with banks around the world, actually raising formative capital was new to him. He admits there were many ups and downs. It was at this time Mr. Griffith was introduced to Paul Kelly, an investment officer at MTDC. MTDC provided early funding which helped attract additional capital, including some from ARD. Eventually MTDC exited Xylogics at a significant gain. Mr. Griffith admitted that the good payoff was very satisfying. After the sale of Xylogics, Mr. Griffith founded College Counsel, where MTDC was again an investor.

The initial MTDC investment in Xylogics was made in April 1980 and exited by IPO in March 1987. The capital return rate was 253% with an IRR of 25.6%, per MTDC reports. The MTDC investment in College Counsel was made in May 1988 and exited by write off in September 1998.[10]

It took several years for MTDC to harvest returns from these initial investments. The original six companies were in the portfolio for the following number of years:

- Spire—4.3
- Discom—8.7
- Xylogics—6.9
- Solenergy—3.1
- Saum—1.2
- Icon—16.6

The total returns in excess of the initial $1,100,000 invested in these six companies, including interest paid and any net capital gains, were over $1 million. Five of the six provided positive returns, and one resulted in a loss.

In addition to financial returns, these companies added new employees and purchased products and services from local suppliers, creating secondary jobs. They also developed products that were "exported" beyond Massachusetts's borders and brought dollars into the Commonwealth. However, most of these initial investments were in early expansion companies that could afford to service debt. The next challenge would be to fund start-up companies.

New Enterprise Formation

In 1981 and 1982, MTDC was able to ramp up its investments in start-up companies. During these years, start-ups added to the portfolio were Aspen, Ikier, Publishing Technology, Interleaf, and Randwal, along with early-expansion companies such as Pacer, Crystal Systems, Proconics, CGX, and Sky Computer. These companies represented the following sectors:

Start-Ups

- Aspen: software for process manufacturers
- Ikier: scientific/engineering workstations
- Publishing Technology: publishing management software
- Interleaf: text-editing software
- Randwal: medical instruments

Expansion

- Pacer: avionics
- Crystal Systems: material science
- Proconics: semiconductor wafer handling systems
- CGX: computer hardware
- Sky Computer: computer hardware

A total of $730,000 was invested among the five start-ups and $1,710,000 among the five early-expansion firms.

Job creation among the start-ups moved at a faster pace than among the early-expansion companies. While the financial risks associated with start-up enterprises were generally higher, the potential rewards were greater. For example, the total net return in excess of the $730,000 invested in the five start-ups was about $3,740,000. On the other hand, for the investment of $1,710,000 in the five expansion firms, the total net return was a loss of about $40,000.

Again, the harvests from the 1981–82 vintage investments took several years: These ten companies were in the portfolio for the following number of years:

- Aspen—9.8
- Ikier—1.7
- Publishing Technology—8.1

- Interleaf—6.8
- Randwal—4.5
- Pacer—4.1
- Crystal Systems—7.8
- Proconics—15.4
- CGX—12.8
- Sky Computer—11

Even the firms from which MTDC realized negative financial returns employed people and brought in dollars to the Massachusetts economy for several years.

During 1983 and the first half of 1984, thirteen new companies were added to the MTDC portfolio: Laser Engineering, Telphi, Vitronics, Fotec, Practek, Computer Solutions, Business Research, Access Technology, Optical Micro, Aeonic, Aseco, Amcard, and Amdev. In addition, follow-on investments were made in five companies.

By June 1984 the portfolio had grown to include a total of twenty-nine companies.

In 1984 MTDC had its first harvest, realizing a gain of $647,000 when new investors and company personnel purchased some of its shares in Interleaf during a second round of financing. Since MTDC had been the only outside investor during the first round, the board decided it would be appropriate to sell some of its shares to new investors. This approach was not typical for private venture capital firms, but consistent with the mission of MTDC as an economic-development agency. It should be noted that the remaining shares of Interleaf were ultimately sold by MTDC when the company went public in 1987 for an additional gain of almost $3 million.

These gains helped to replenish the investment fund and underwrite operational expenses. As it turned out, these investment harvests became critical since 1987 was the last year that the MTDC received any appropriation from the Commonwealth and no additional federal funds had been received since 1980.

Metrics of Success

In addition to developing an effective investment process and launching a sizable and diversified portfolio of investments, the MTDC began to track the amount of private dollars that were coinvested in the initial round of financing. For the fiscal year 1984, initial private dollars leveraged were about $4 for each $1 from MTDC. In later years, the number of jobs among portfolio companies was monitored. For example, in FY87, there were over 2,500 jobs, with a total annual payroll in excess of $77 million, among thirty-five active companies. Dollars leveraged and jobs became key statistics that helped to document how well MTDC was accomplishing its economic-development mission.

Cumulative realized net gains were also very important, even though the enabling charter only specified "there is a reasonable possibility that the MTDC will recoup at least its initial investment." The practical reality was that MTDC had to demonstrate financial success in order to attract private coinvestors and to finance its own operations and investment budget.

Transitional Year

In 1984, William Aikman, who had become president and CEO of the MTDC in 1980, decided to resign and join a newly established venture capital partnership. In addition, three of the four members of the investment staff, Paul Ballantine, Robert Lepkowski, and Stephen McCormack, had resigned to take private-sector venture capital jobs. The early track record of MTDC had earned its staff a reputation of being well-trained venture capital professionals, and the corporation was viewed as a good source of talent for the expanding venture capital industry in Boston.

In July 1984, I was hired as the new president and CEO of MTDC.

CHAPTER 2
GROWING THE CORPORATION

Relaunching the Enterprise

My experiences before joining MTDC included nine years as a human resource manager with a "Big 8" accounting firm, two years as the CEO of a large state agency, three years as the CEO of an early-stage software company, and one year as a management consultant and entrepreneur. I found that every one of these jobs had great relevance as the new leader of the MTDC.

The first challenge was to build up a new investment staff. Just before I joined MTDC, the board had elected Robert Crowley, the one remaining member of the previous investment staff, to be the corporation's vice president. Bob was a former commercial bank loan officer who had joined the MTDC after it was established in 1978. His role had been to develop investment prospects, and he had been very successful in this job.

During my first meeting with Bob, he affirmed his commitment to the mission of the corporation and said he would provide the continuity necessary to maintain its early success. I concluded immediately that I would work to make Bob my partner in the endeavor.

Bob had hired Barbara Plantholt, a former commercial bank lending officer, as a consultant a short time before I started. He and Barbara had taken over the responsibility of monitoring the twenty-nine companies in the portfolio and beginning to identify prospective new investments. However, we needed to augment the staff in the very near term.

My experience as a personnel manager with a "Big 8" accounting firm had shown me that a strategy of hiring high-potential but less experienced people, training and coaching them systematically, and assigning responsibility early could be successful. Furthermore, the compensation levels at MTDC precluded hiring experienced venture capital investment professionals. The corporation had just lost its previous president and three of its investment staff to other firms paying substantially higher salaries.

In the next few months we hired Jeff Davison, Laura Morrisette, and Jeff Wallace. All had some previous business experience, mostly in lending to smaller companies. They were also bright, curious, and good communicators, who appeared to be very interested in learning the practice of venture capital while working with innovative technology-based companies.

While I had over fifteen years of leadership and management experience, I needed to learn the venture capital process. Bob Crowley and several members of the board became very valuable mentors. The challenge of training new staff members required me to rapidly learn the vocabulary and concepts of venture financing.

I also learned very quickly about the human element in venture capital investing. Within the first three months of my joining the MTDC, Bob Crowley suggested that I visit a company that had applied for an investment. The firm was Snell Acoustics, and I was to meet with its founder, a young man named Peter Snell. Our meeting in the company's factory had just started when Mr. Snell collapsed. It turned out that he had a fatal heart attack. This tragic event underscored how important the entrepreneur was to the success of the enterprise. While the company continued to operate, it had lost its founder and key product designer. This experience would be repeated again in 2001, when the founder of one of the MTDC's newer investments was a victim in the 9/11 terrorist attacks. However, in the latter case, the company did not survive.

Technology Trends

In addition to learning the basics of venture capital investing, I had to develop an understanding of longer-term trends that would lead to innovations based on the application of technology. One of these trends was the increasing power and decreasing cost of computer technology. By the early 1980s, two fundamental technological developments launched the widespread use of computers in every part of daily life. These were the introduction of relatively low-cost personal computers and the development and sale of software independent from hardware.

Apple and many other new computer companies had introduced personal computers in the late 1970s. However, it was IBM that brought out its standard-setting product in 1981. The operating system software that ran the IBM personal computer and those from other computer hardware companies was MS- DOS. This software, independent from hardware, became the foundation product of Microsoft.

The challenge was how to communicate to the public that these new tools were available and could be used by anyone. In 1981 IBM ran TV ads using the Charlie Chaplin character of the tramp. The tramp opened a box containing a microcomputer and proceeded to use it. The ad conveyed the notion that anyone could now take advantage of this new technology.[11]

In 1984, Hewlett Packard (HP) introduced a personal computer that had a keyboard, but also employed touch-screen technology. The idea was that executives and managers would not be willing to use the keyboard since that was a tool of secretaries. Very soon it became clear that most senior executives and managers were not going to use PCs. However, younger staff members were quite willing to use keyboards. The personal computer became the new desktop tool in corporations, to the great frustration of many of their IT departments.

Also in 1984, Apple introduced the Macintosh, revolutionizing how ordinary people would interact with computers. Its graphical user interface (GUI) became the standard. Microsoft later adopted a similar GUI approach with its Windows operating system.

While minicomputers from companies like Digital Equipment (DEC), HP, and Data General were the dominant platforms in medium to smaller enterprises, desktop workstations were beginning to show up everywhere. For example, when I joined the MTDC in 1984, the corporation had purchased several DEC Rainbow desktop computers that were running Microsoft's DOS operating system software. However, apart from accounting, these were not used very much by the investment staff to write reports or do spreadsheet analyses.

With more users of both minicomputer and desktop workstations, there was a greater demand for applications software, making these tools useful to workers at every level of most enterprises. Word processing was proliferating in large and medium-sized companies. Wang Laboratories in Lowell emerged as a leading provider of this application. A new company, Lotus 123 in Cambridge, became a leader in providing spreadsheet applications. And Apple hardware and software emerged as the leader in the graphic design sector.

Niche Market Opportunities

It seemed that the MTDC would be better suited to identify and help finance new companies bringing innovative uses of technology to emerging market niches. Given the amount of money the corporation could invest, even with a four-to-one ratio of private coinvestment, the total amount invested in an initial round might be between $1 and $2 million per company. This level of investment would be better suited for smaller niches, not huge, game-changing market opportunities. These smaller market niches were not as attractive to competitors from larger well-financed corporations. The trick was to find entrepreneurs who had specialized knowledge and skills in both the technologies and market niches in which they would be applied.

Between the summer of 1984 and the winter of 1985, the MTDC investment staff identified a few of these niche market players. One company was Wakefield Software Systems, which focused on software to read bar codes and manage these data. At the time, the use of bar coding was expanding, but it was not yet ubiquitous. Another was Geographic Systems, a very early provider of geographic information systems (GIS) software that ran on DEC minicomputers. This software was used for marketing decision analysis in medium to larger enterprises. The third was Cambridge Analytic, a laboratory that focused its analytic tools and services to respond to the growing need to identify and remediate hazardous waste sites. Finally, Chromatic Technologies focused on the manufacturing of specialized fiber-optical cabling for especially hostile environments.

Another type of investment target was an existing company that was rejuvenating its business by bringing out new technology-based products. During the summer of 1985, MTDC invested in Zoom Telephonics. This firm had grown very fast by offering a programmable dialer that enabled customers to access alternative long-distance phone carriers. However, once the regulations changed and made this product unnecessary, Zoom shifted into developing and selling a product line of dial-up modems.

The Frank Manning story was reported as follows by Rob Frohman:

Frank Manning—Zoom Telephonics

Frank Manning provides a fine example of disruptive innovation for a single entrepreneur and within a single company. Mr. Manning leads Zoom Telephonics, which has seen significant change in the market and its products during his tenure. He demonstrates the tenacity and resilience very typical of technology entrepreneurs. As well, he reflects an entrepreneurial ethic which stemmed from his youth, with his father setting the bar: "Have your own business."

Mr. Manning earned his Ph.D., M.Sc., and B.Sc. from the Massachusetts Institute of Technology, where he was also a National Science Foundation Fellow. As a graduate student, Mr. Manning and his roommate Bruce Kramer faced a problem. Tennis court reservations were made on a first-come first-serve basis, and the telephone lines opened at noon. Often finding it difficult to get through to make the reservation, the pair developed an automated tone-hearing dialer to be sure to get through fast.

In 1977, Mr. Manning formed Zoom with Bruce Kramer, Bruce's bother Peter and Frank's brother T. Patrick Manning, and Zoom introduced its first product, the Silencer. This product was a switch that could be attached to a telephone to prevent ringing.

The Silencer generated about $200k per year and was the focus of Mr. Manning's "Day Job." At night, he continued to work on the Demon Dialer through 1981. With the introduction of long-distance telephone companies like MCI and Sprint, competing with AT & T, customers were required to dial up to 23 numbers to reach these networks. The Demon Dialer could store and dial numbers up to 32 digits long, hear call progress tones, and work for all the phones on a line, simplifying access to these networks for home and office. With the success of the product, Zoom grew rapidly from $200k to $6 million. As well, in this period, Zoom took on much debt, increased its payroll, and built up much inventory.

When the dialer market was booming, Mr. Manning had been introduced to MTDC through the Bank of Boston. When moderating the MIT Enterprise Forum, MTDC Vice President and Chief Investment Officer Bob Crowley identified Zoom's presentation as having the "Most positive spin on an undercapitalized company." At that time Zoom was concerned about share dilution and was not willing to partner with MTDC.

After initial rapid dialer market growth, the advent of "equal access" meant that alternate long distance no longer required dialing 23 digits, severely hurting dialer sales. Mr. Manning recounted this is where Zoom "Got smart and lucky," licensing 300 baud modems for the Apple II computer. This launched a significant business for Zoom, but first Zoom had to work through the problems of a crashing dialer market and a nervous bank. At a Massachusetts event honoring Zoom and other Inc. 500 Fastest Growing Companies, Mr. Manning saw Bob Crowley and asked for help. Mr. Crowley immediately introduced MTDC President John Hodgman; and MTDC did rapid, thorough due diligence that resulted in an investment. MTDC also provided other support, giving business guidance and helping with Zoom's bank and with Zoom's largest supplier. MTDC's rapid response to Zoom's needs was crucial to Zoom's success.

Zoom grew its modem business to $100 million per year of profitable sales, going public in 1988. Years later, Mr. Manning participated as a member of the MTDC board to help thank MTDC and to bring its benefits to enterprising young Massachusetts companies. Mr. Manning enjoyed working on the board because of MIT's mission, its talented staff and board, and the excellent young companies MTDC considered for investment.

Mr. Manning demonstrated the true technologist to entrepreneur story. He enjoyed learning business thorough real-world experience. As is common with technology entrepreneurs, Mr. Manning's interest went beyond technology into marketing, finance, operations, and the other areas of business so important to success. He advocates strongly that both funding and good advice are critical for a young technology startup.

An initial MTDC investment was made in August 1985 and MTDC exited in March 1992 with a capital return rate of 979% and an IRR of 52.7%, per MTDC reports.[12]

Ultimately, from these five niche companies, the MTDC realized gains in three cases and losses in two. However, during the four to seven years that each company was in the portfolio, they collectively employed over 400 people and helped to create and maintain 800 to 1,200 secondary jobs from local suppliers. Over this period the MTDC staff were active at the board-of-director level with each of these companies, focusing especially on their financing needs.

Financial Conditions

In the early 1980s, interest rates were at extraordinary high levels. For example, in order to arrest annual inflation rates in excess of 10 percent, the Federal Reserve raised the prime interest rate to a high of 21.5 percent in June 1982. This influenced the interest rates at which companies could borrow money and what banks had to pay for certificates of deposit (CD).

During its early years, the MTDC was restricted to making loans from the funds provided by the federal government. Most of these loans had interest rates in excess of 15 percent. In addition, there were equity features attached to the loans, such as stock purchase warrants, to compensate for the risks associated with early-stage technology companies. The interest income from these loans generated substantial cash that helped to underwrite the operating expenses of the corporation. Furthermore, interest income from cash held in bank accounts not yet invested in companies was also substantial. For example, as late as 1984 and 1985, interest rates on CDs ranged from 8 percent to 11 percent.

Investors could reap these high interest-rate returns without taking the risk of making equity investment in early-stage companies. The "Reagan Recession" of 1981–82 also constrained investors' appetites. Consequently, the amount of equity risk capital was in relatively short supply. However, as the economy began to recover, the rate of inflation began to decrease. For example, the unemployment rate decreased from a high of 10.8 percent in December 1982 to 7.2 percent by November 1984. The inflation rate dropped from 10.3 percent in 1981 to 3.2 percent in 1983. By the mid-1980s, the flow of equity risk capital began to increase.

Fire, Flood, and PCs

While on a long Labor Day weekend trip, I saw on the morning TV news broadcast that a fire being reported looked like it was in the building where MTDC had its office. I knew we had a big problem. However, since the fire happened on the weekend, I believed that no one was likely to have been injured. I returned immediately to Boston and discovered that the fire was in the office a floor above MTDC's at 84 State Street. While we did not have any fire damage, the water from the sprinkler system and fire hoses had completely flooded our suite. Most of the furniture, as well as all of our computers and other office equipment, were a total loss. Fortunately, most of our paper files were intact.

After calling upon one of our "sister" economic-development agencies, the Community Development Finance Corporation (CDFC), for help, we were invited to use a couple of rooms in their office for a few days. Within weeks another "sister," the Massachusetts Industrial Finance Agency (MIFA), sublet us temporary office space in a building from which they had recently moved, but where their lease had not yet expired. MTDC was back in business in a couple of weeks. Within a few months, our office had been renovated, and we moved back to 84 State Street.

We had to decide what type of desktop computers we would purchase to replace the DEC Rainbows. While a year before I had purchased a first-generation Apple Macintosh for my home and was very pleased with its intuitive human interface and design, we decided to go with PCs and Windows. At the time, the Mac did not support as much business software as Windows. It would be over twenty-three years before I returned to the Mac as my preferred computer.

MTDC and PRIT

Since the original $10 million of investment capital for the MTDC was not appropriated when the corporation was created in 1978, a few years later some legislative supporters tried to come up with a creative solution. In 1983, the Massachusetts Pension Reserve Investment Trust (PRIT) was created to address the large unfunded pension liability of the Commonwealth. A new entity, the Massachusetts Pension Reserve Investment Management (PRIM) Board, was formed to oversee PRIT. The enabling law included a provision that the MTDC would manage $2 million on behalf of PRIT.

The PRIM board and staff were all newcomers to the role of investing the pension reserve funds contributed by the Commonwealth as an employer. Previously, most pension contributions were deducted from the paychecks of individual state employees and teachers. Now the additional employer contributions would help to address the unfunded pension liability of the Commonwealth and many of its subsidiary organizations.

The chairman of the PRIM board was State Treasurer Robert Crane, a long-serving elected official who was not a professional investment executive, but a very savvy politician. The new executive director of PRIM, Paul Quirk, had a long labor-union background, but was also not a professional investment executive. Furthermore, most of the initial PRIM top staff members were inexperienced in the investment field.

At one of the earliest meetings I attended with the treasurer, Mr. Quirk, and others in the leadership of PRIM, the agenda included a discussion of the legislative mandate that MTDC manage $2 million of the PRIT funds. Mr. Crane asked whether they really had to honor this requirement. My answer was that the MTDC would not want to undertake this commitment unless we could reach a mutually satisfactory agreement.

The agreement would have to include specific language as to the investment goals and criteria for these funds. All of the investments would be in Massachusetts early-stage technology companies, helping to create new jobs in the Commonwealth. However, the basic objective would be to achieve high financial returns. In effect, MTDC would become one of the first venture capital investment managers in the history of the PRIT.

The PRIM board hired Wilshire Associates from California as its investment advisor. Doug LeBon of Wilshire was assigned the task of reviewing MTDC's investment history and plan. After several months, an agreement between MTDC and PRIM was signed, and the first investments were made in 1986.

The MTDC-PRIT portfolio added the following companies:

- Aeonic Systems (1986)
- Aseco Corporation (1986)
- Business Research (1986)
- Kronos Inc. (1987)
- Voicetek (1987)
- Sky Computer (1988)
- IMC Systems (1989)
- IVS Inc. (1989)
- Cimtelligence (1990)
- Multilink, Inc. (1992)

Among these companies were early innovators in areas such as

- computerized process-control systems—Aeonic;
- computer test-handling systems—Aseco;
- online investment-research systems—Business Research; and
- voice messaging and processing systems—Voicetek.

Of these ten investments, four yielded returns in excess of 200 percent, one yielded in excess of 167 percent, four were partial losses, and one was a total loss. By the time this investment agreement ended in the early 1990s, all of the original $2 million plus $750,000 in gains had been returned to PRIT.

MTDC Traditional Fund

During the late 1980s, the MTDC added the following companies to its Traditional Fund portfolio:

- Microtouch Systems Inc. (1986)
- XRL Inc. (1987)
- Amherst Electronic Inc. (1987)
- Harbor Medical Devices (1987)
- Cramer Interactive Video (1987)
- Tytronics Inc. (1987)
- IMC Systems Group (1987)
- Multilink Inc. (1987)
- Spectrovision Inc. (1987)
- College Counsel, Inc. (1987)
- Data Innovation Inc. (1988)
- IVS, Inc. (1988)
- Millitech Corp. (1988)
- Voicetek (1988)

Among these companies were "pioneers" in the development of new technology-based innovations that later became well-established in larger markets. For example, Microtouch was one of the early providers of touch screens used by a wide array of businesses to interact with customers. Multilink was an early leader in providing teleconferencing systems.

Most of the funds to make these investments came from the repayments of loans, returns of capital, and realized gains, in particular over $3 million from Interleaf after its public offering in 1987. In addition, the Commonwealth had added $1.4 million to the investment fund between 1986 and 1987.

I found it interesting that in 1986 Microtouch had developed applications for touch-screen technology, which had been a bust for Hewlett Packard in 1984. This would not be the first time I witnessed the repositioning of a technology from a losing application to those that would be profitable.

The following stories from two of the MTDC entrepreneurs help to provide background about the investment climate during the late 1980s. Both Josh Tolkoff and Paul Gasparro became serial entrepreneurs. In more recent years, Josh became a venture investor and a mentor to young entrepreneurs. His comment about the relatively slower investment process by the MTDC may be a result of this experience. However, the thorough due-diligence process of the MTDC was required by its charter and has stood the test of time.

These two entrepreneurs cofounded Harbor Medical Devices and Voicetek, respectively. Their stories were reported by Rob Frohman as follows:

Josh Tolkoff—Harbor Medical Devices

Always having an interest in technology, Josh Tolkoff received a degree from Harvard in Engineering &

Applied Physics and then went onto M.I.T to receive a M. Sc. in Biomechanics. Mr. Tolkoff started work in industry for 3 years, then returned to research at MGH working on new devices for clinical researchers. He joined Medi-Tech as the head of Research and Development. Medi-Tech became Boston Scientific and he helped grow the company from 20 to 500 employees.

Mr. Tolkoff left Boston Scientific to launch his first startup, Harbor Medical Devices, which developed implantable access devices for chemotherapy. MTDC was an early investor providing $620,000 in funding, with Harbor Medical eventually raising a total of $3 million in 9 to 12 months. Harbor Medical was the type of company MTDC liked to invest in, providing capital that would help secure additional investment.

Mr. Tolkoff enjoyed working with MTDC, seeing the people he worked with as smart advisors in spite of being early in their careers. As a result, they did not often stay long resulting in churn on the staff. As Mr. Tolkoff recounted, having investors with only investment management experience on the board of a startup was not optimal. He preferred more operating experiencing board members. While short in tenure, the MTDC staff members knew the technology startup space. In addition, they were well connected and highly diligent.

Harbor Medical was eventually unsuccessful, due to issues in the market. Mr. Tolkoff, a serial entrepreneur, moved to his next startup, ACT Medical, a medical contract developer and manufacturer. Within 8 years, ACT Medical was employing 200 people, dividing its business across contract development and manufacturing. As Mr. Tolkoff remarked about the transitions, "Lots have the head and the heart, but not the stomach for startups." ACT Medical was acquired by MedSource Technologies and Mr. Tolkoff moved on, largely preferring to work with early stage companies.

Mr. Tolkoff enjoyed working with MTDC however recommended that there are issues today due to its low capitalization. It operated like any other VC but the vetting process resulted in a slower approval process and that it could benefit from a more streamlined approach.[13]

Paul Gasparro—Voicetek

Paul Gasparro is a serial entrepreneur, founding several companies in the communications industry. He received a B.Sc. in Electrical Engineering from the University of Illinois and an M.B.A several years later from the Illinois Institute of Technology.

Mr. Gasparro started his career in product development at Motorola then moved onto Fairchild exploring voicemail solutions in 1983. With an interest in business, Mr. Gasparro returned to school to pursue an M.B.A to gain the education he needed to "leverage those skills." Starting in sales at Fairchild, he moved up quickly to run a Fairchild division. While leading the division at Fairchild, Mr. Gasparro was interested in exploring options on how to break out to focus on the voicemail market. He contacted a recruiter who proposed he join an Interactive Voice Response incubator. He chose to join and worked in the basement of the building where day-to-day details fell to him to solve.

A challenge facing Voicetek was that a partner had 80% ownership of the company, so venture capital was not very interested in making a commitment. Mr. Gasparro recalled the challenges of raising capital. He was unfamiliar with the process, digging into research and using any resource available to him. Writing the business plan was a difficult task, finding his network critical in aiding him in the effort. He admitted waiting to hear the result from investors was especially difficult. Regardless, Mr. Gasparro had no real fear of failure.

The company had 4 executives, 25 employees, and 1 customer and the company was pursuing its first round of funding when Mr. Gasparro was introduced to John Hodgman and Bob Crowley. The opportunity was met by MTDC and an investment was made, just before the market crash of 1987 [sic]. Mr. Gasparro found MTDC to be process oriented, observing that venture capital has a tendency to go more by gut. Though the overhead may have been painful at times, he found it useful. When asked about plan execution, Mr. Gasparro commented that it was not even close, that things change.

Mr. Gasparro sees his relationship with MTDC as a good one. The quasi-public aspects were not an issue, though he offered that the process might be too stringent.

An initial MTDC investment was made in December 1988 and exited through the sale of the company in May 2000 achieving a capital return rate of 427% and an IRR of 19.9%, per MTDC reports.[14]

Signs of Success

By early 1987, several of the investments MTDC had made in the early 1980s started to yield financial returns. In addition to Interleaf, CAA, DISCOM, Vitronics, and Xylogics had gone public. The net gains, return on invested capital, repayments of loans, interest earned, and additional funds from the Commonwealth had increased the total cash available in the corporation's treasury from about $4.3 million at the end of 1986 to about $6.9 million by May 1987.

By June 1987, the total number of jobs among the still-active companies that MTDC had helped to finance had reached over 2,800. At the time, the top four employers in the portfolio were

- Interleaf (355);
- Access Technology (123);
- DISCOM (114); and
- Cambridge Analytic Associates (97).

Among the former portfolio companies, the top four employers were

- Pacer Systems (450);
- Xylogics (193);
- Spire (164); and
- Business Research (134).

The aggregate employment among these small emerging companies made this group one of the larger private-sector employers in the Commonwealth. Governor Weld once said that in order to revitalize the Massachusetts economy, it would take an "army of ants." The MTDC portfolio represented a division of this army.

Another metric of success was that for every $1 MTDC invested, there were $4 to $5 of initial coinvestments from private-sector venture capital firms, individuals, and corporations. In most cases, MTDC had been the catalyst for investments in these companies, "the first olive out of the bottle." The MTDC had become a respected player in the start-up and early-stage technology venture investing marketplace.

The relaunch of the corporation had been successful, and it was poised to ramp up its effort in the next fiscal year, ending on June 30, 1988.

Model for Other Regions

By 1987, the MTDC had become recognized by both government and private-sector leaders in regions around the world and the United States as a successful model to help create new companies and jobs. Its reputation had been spread through articles published in newspapers and journals. In addition, Economic Innovation International, Inc. (EII), a consulting firm that worked with government and civic groups in a number of regions, often pointed to the MTDC. There was a long history of EII's relationship with the MTDC.

The executive director of the governor's Capital Formation Task Force that recommended the creation of the MTDC in 1976–77 was Belden Daniels. At the time, he was teaching development finance at the Harvard Graduate School of Design and the Kennedy School. Belden had also formed Economic Innovation International, Inc. in 1970. The following quote from its website summarizes the focus and history of this consulting firm.

> Economic Innovation International, founded in 1970, is now internationally recognized for building more than $150 billion of privately capitalized innovative institutions to accomplish public purposes in North America, Europe and Asia. These funds generate measurable wealth and high quality jobs for low income

> residents of targeted communities in emerging markets. During the last decade, these Triple Bottom Line, mission-driven funds have become fully green.
>
> Regional economies, like nations, live in a world of constant change, increasing competition, and economic and cultural dynamism. Economic Innovation helps communities design and build realistic action plans, funds and institutions that increase their current comparative economic advantage and strengthen their underlying human, financial, and technological resources. Economic Innovation's overarching goal with each client is to help advance smart communities, smart enterprises, and smart workers who can compete in today's global technology-driven economy.[15]

In June 2014, Belden Daniels sent me an e-mail in which he reported how his experience with the MTDC influenced the establishment of venture investment organizations that had the goal of stimulating economic development.

> Economic Innovation went on to help design and build 26 technology commercialization, seed capital and venture capital funds modeled on MTDC with more than $3.2 Billion in capital committed. These include:

- the Polaris Fund of Alaska (1981),
- the Arkansas Science & Technology Authority (1985),
- the (San Francisco) Bay Area Equity Fund I (California 2004),
- Connecticut Innovations, Inc. (1988),
- Connecticut Seed Capital Venture Fund (1988),
- Enterprise Florida Innovation Partnership (1994),
- Enterprise Florida Cypress Equity Fund (1994)
- Kansas Technology Enterprise Corporation (1986),

- Mid-America Manufacturing Technology Center (1986),
- Kansas Venture Capital, Inc. (1986),
- Ad Astra Seed Capital Fund (Kansas, 1988),
- Kentucky Science & Technology Council (1987),
- Louisiana Science and Technology Foundation (1984),
- Louisiana Seed Capital Corporation (1984),
- Louisiana Partnership for Technology and Innovation (1984),
- Louisiana Renewable Resources Foundation (1984),
- Maine Science & Technology (1995),
- St. Louis Missouri Vectis Fund I (2005),
- St. Louis Missouri Vectis Fund II (2008),
- Nebraska Research and Development Corporation (1983),
- Nebraska Heartland Capital Partners (1987),
- Oklahoma Center for the Advancement of Science & Technology (1987),
- Oregon Resource & Technology Development Fund (1984),
- the Palestine Information and Communications Technology Corporation (2004),
- Plock Technology Development Center (Poland, 1993) and
- the Virginia Center for Innovative Technology (1996).[16]

MTDC Visitors

Between FY85 and FY87, visitors from sixteen countries and twelve states came to the MTDC. Different teams from France came five times. There were four different visits from teams from Spain and England. Germany, Australia, Brazil, and Canada each represented three visits. Two each came from the Netherlands and Japan. Finally, the following countries had teams that each made one visit: Belgium, Norway, Korea, Sweden, Taiwan, Italy, and Greece. China had not yet opened up, so teams from this country did not begin to appear until the 1990s.

In terms of states, Colorado and Texas each had two different teams who visited. The following each had one visit: Illinois, North Carolina, Utah, Oklahoma, District of Columbia, Hawaii, California, Oregon, Rhode Island, and Arkansas.

The number of states that visited would pick up significantly in FY88, the year in which Governor Dukakis was running for president. During that fiscal year, there were teams that visited from Iowa, Colorado, Montana (twice), Idaho, Wisconsin, Georgia, and Delaware. There were also twenty-one different teams from fifteen countries that visited in FY88. There was great interest in learning what made Massachusetts's innovation economy successful.

The Massachusetts environment for technology start-ups has been in the top ranking after Silicon Valley as measured by the amount of venture capital investments. However, the capital gap for very small niche market-focused technology start-ups has been chronic since the 1970s. MTDC's success in addressing the needs of these types of companies seemed to be most relevant to those regions of the United States and the world where the venture capital infrastructure had not been developed.

China

In 1988, the Tufts Fletcher School managed a program to train Chinese middle managers in business. The US Agency for International Development had funded a grant to bring these managers to study at Tufts for a year, as well as to experience an internship with a US firm. Two of these managers were recommended to me for an internship with the MTDC.

Keming Zhang and Lin Rong spent several weeks with the corporation over the winter of 1998–1989. They worked on an analysis of the potential for several selected MTDC portfolio companies to export their products to China. This was at a time when the Chinese economy was just beginning to experiment with some "capitalistic" business strategies.

After successfully completing the project, Keming Zhang and Lin Rong were preparing to return to China in June 1989. However, the Tiananmen Square protest suppression that took place that month altered their plans. They did not know whether it would be safe for them to return since they were among the young men and women being exposed to American democracy and business.

Lin Rong learned that the new head of the Party and government of China was a former mayor of Shanghai. He had worked in the mayor's office in that city and had connections that provided some assurances, so he went back to China that summer.

Keming Zhang was a younger man, who did not have the same level of comfort about returning and felt he would like to stay in the United States. During the summer of 1989, he continued his internship with the MTDC, and I introduced him to one of our coinvestors, Tom Claflin. I knew that Tom had started a small fund to invest in companies in China and thought Keming could be helpful. By the fall, Keming joined Tom's firm full-time and began his apprenticeship as an investment manager.

Eventually, Keming began to focus exclusively on managing the China investment funds for the firm. He married Grace, a Chinese woman who had emigrated to the United States and became a tax accountant. Their two sons were born in the United States. Later the family moved back to China for part of each year. Keming anglicized his name to Fred and continues to manage the investment funds. In the last few years, the family returned to reside permanently in Boston.

When I first met the two Chinese interns, I had a vague sense that China's economy was about to grow rapidly. The Tiananmen Square episode portended a major setback. However, twenty-five years later, China has become an economic powerhouse, and has become linked to the United States in ways that seemed unimaginable during 1989.

CHAPTER 3

BECOMING SELF-SUSTAINING

MTDC Board of Directors

Among the key factors contributing to the success of the MTDC, one of the most important was the quality of the members of the board of directors. The eight private-sector members who were appointed by the governor were an extraordinary group of savvy volunteers who wanted to give back by helping the next generation of entrepreneurs.

The first group of directors was shaped by the culture of the volunteer board members of MTDC's predecessor, the Massachusetts Science and Technology Foundation (MSTF). They were committed to the mission and very sensitive to the duties of honest public service.

When I joined MTDC in 1984, the private-sector members of the board were

- Howard Smith, chairman, a CEO of several companies and former secretary of economic affairs of the Commonwealth;
- John Ehrenfeld, an entrepreneur in the field of environmental sustainability;
- Joseph Iandiorio, a patent attorney and business advisor;

- Timothy McNeill, a management consultant;
- Judith Obermayer, an entrepreneur, investor, and counselor to young companies;
- Robert Seamans, a faculty member and dean of MIT, and former secretary of the air force; and
- Phyllis Sherry Swersky, a senior executive with a leading software company.

There was one private-sector vacancy that would later be filled by the governor.

The three public-sector members of the board were senior officials of the Commonwealth, including the lieutenant governor, the secretary of administration and finance, and the secretary of economic affairs. In recognition of the roles and responsibilities of these officials, MTDC's charter permitted them to send designees to act in their place at board meetings. As a result, a group of senior deputies to these officials became consistent contributors. In 1984, these designees included:

James Gomes, representing Lt. Governor John Kerry;

B. J. Rudman, representing Secretary of Administration and Finance Frank Keefe; and

Joseph Baerline, representing Secretary of Economic Affairs Evelyn Murphy.

Investment Process

The MTDC enabling law stipulated that any investment decision required the approval of at least six members of the board. Furthermore, the board had to make specific findings before granting approval. These findings are detailed in chapter 1. While confidential information about specific companies was exempted from the freedom-of-public-information requirements, the investment process had to be transparent. Therefore, a systematic and consistent process was essential. While some entrepreneurs might have viewed it as cumbersome, it became a valued methodology that helped to attract private coinvestors. When MTDC approved a deal, it was viewed to have been thoroughly vetted.

MTDC Staffing Model

While the compensation levels for investment professionals was considerably less than in private venture capital firms, the opportunity to learn to how to become a venture professional was attractive. Therefore, the MTDC was able to recruit high-caliber new investment personnel who wanted to enter the venture capital field.

The MTDC developed a very good reputation for training newer investment staff members. As a result, private venture capital firms often recruited these individuals after they had several years of experience. These "alumni" helped to strengthen the network of potential coinvestors.

The officers of MTDC, especially Bob Crowley and I, and many of the support staff—Gail Cormier, Esther Larson, Marie Phaneuf, Mary Stack, and Karen Butts—worked together for many years. This core team provided continuity that made the turnover of investment staff members less disruptive.

Boom to Bust

During July 1987 the operating plan for FY88 approved by the board called for $2.8 million to be invested in nine to twelve companies new to the MTDC portfolio; $600, 000 of PRIT funds to be invested in three companies; and five full-time-equivalent investment professionals. There was also the potential to augment the management-assistance program if the proposed additional $100,000 in the state budget was approved. The plans also assumed the addition of $800,000 for the investment fund, which was also in the state budget.

This plan was adopted when there were general expectations of a very robust environment for new enterprises. For example, earlier in the spring of 1987, Governor Dukakis had announced "Creating the Future" as his administration's innovation initiative. This plan called for the following:

1. Creation of a Center for Applied Technology and Productivity at UMASS Amherst and Lowell, as well as at Worcester Polytechnic Institute, that would be part of the Massachusetts Centers of Excellence Corporation (MCEC);
2. Publicly funded business incubators through the Massachusetts Government Land Bank;
3. A "Marketing Massachusetts" campaign in conjunction with the Massachusetts Software Council;
4. Support for SBIR award winners through bridge funds administered by the MCEC and technical advice provided by the MTDC; and
5. "Massachusetts Jobs Southeast," which would provide customized job training for personnel working for private employers.[17]

In March 1987, the *Wall Street Journal* reported that the venture capital firm Warburg Pincus had raised the largest fund ever in the entire industry, $1.17 billion.[18] This event symbolized the expectations of many venture capital firms that there would be abundant investment opportunities ahead.

There were few signs that the stock market was about to crash in October 1987. On "Black Monday," October 19, 1987, worldwide stock markets began to fall, starting in Hong Kong, then spreading west to Europe and finally to the United States. The Dow Jones Industrial Average fell by 22.6 percent to 1,739, and did not return to its August 1987 closing high of 2,722 until two years later. While the stock markets stabilized, the window for initial public offerings closed and did not open widely again until 1991. Since this was the most profitable exit strategy for venture-backed companies, investment returns of venture capital partnerships also suffered.

Another development in 1987 was that Governor Dukakis was beginning to take steps to run for president in 1988. A strong point in his campaign would be the strength of the Massachusetts economy, which began to be called the "Massachusetts Miracle." However, the early signs of an economic decline appeared when the state began to see less revenue in FY88 than was projected in the budget.

In December 1987, the early indicator that the FY88 budget deficit would impact the MTDC appeared when we learned that the governor's FY89 budget would not include any additional investment funds for the corporation. The original plan in 1978 to capitalize the MTDC with $10 million was about to fall short. Only a total of $8.2 million had been placed in the investment fund, and of that $3 million came from the federal government. Coincidently, in October 1987, the MTDC was notified by the federal agency that administered the first $2 million that the grant requirements had been successfully accomplished and no further progress reports had to be submitted.

While the lack of new investment funds in the governor's budget was a concern, the MTDC had begun to realize significant gains that could be used to fund new companies. During FY87, MTDC realized gains of $3.7 million, most of which were a result of the successful IPO of

Interleaf. As of the end of November 1987, the corporation had almost $6.8 million in cash.

Shift in Investment Strategy

While there were ample funds to continue to invest in new companies, it now became apparent that more money would have to be allocated for follow-on investments in the existing portfolio. Venture capital investing in new deals was beginning to dry up. MTDC could not expect its companies to be able to raise follow-on rounds from new investors to the same degree as in past years.

At the September 1987 meeting, the MTDC board had approved investments in two new companies: Data Innovation and Spectrovision. In October, an investment in Voicetek from the PRIT fund was approved. An investment in College Counsel was approved in November. Then, as we entered 1988, the pace of new company investments began to slow. No new investment recommendations were made at the February and March board meetings. In April, Cayman Systems was approved, but this investment was not closed since the company had received other financing.

By the end of February 1988, there was about $3 million of cash that was not yet committed to investments, and another $2.4 in reserves. However, the prospect for near-term harvests was not good. The IPO window was closed, and it would take more time for portfolio companies to mature before they were candidates for acquisition by larger companies.

Settling Up with the Commonwealth

In early June 1988, I received a phone call from Frank Keefe, the secretary of administration and finance and an ex officio member of the MTDC board. His designee, B. J. Rudman, had been representing him at the meetings and was well-aware of the status of the MTDC's treasury. Secretary Keefe's message was that the Commonwealth's FY88 budget had a large deficit, and he was asking all of the quasi-public corporations to contribute to filling the gap. Not only would there be no additional funds in FY89, but the Commonwealth wanted to be repaid for funds that were appropriated for MTDC and its predecessor, the Massachusetts Science and Technology Foundation (MSTF).

Between FY69 and FY88, the Commonwealth had appropriated operating funds for the MSTF totaling $1.2 million and $1.5 million for the MTDC. This total of $2.7 million had funded average annual operating expenses of $142,000 over each of the nineteen years.

The requirement to repay these funds was qualified by the Massachusetts attorney general. In 1972, six years before the creation of the MTDC, the attorney general rendered an opinion about the funds appropriated for the MSTF that said "such continued funding by the Commonwealth suggests that the Legislature is mindful that the Foundation requires state support until such time as it is able to be self-supporting."[19] This statement was included in the footnote section in each of the MTDC annual financial statements between 1978 and 1987.

The secretary of administration and finance had now made the judgment that the MTDC was self-supporting and it should reimburse the Commonwealth. Of course, the MTDC was a wholly owned entity of the state, so the reimbursement would be from "one pocket to another."

When I reviewed Secretary Keefe's request with my colleague Bob Crowley, he suggested that we propose to make a payment to the Commonwealth and ask Secretary Keefe if he would file legislation to have this payment fully discharge any obligation to repay the remaining balance owed. We recommended to the MTDC board that the corporation pay $750,000 to the Commonwealth. This was an amount that would leave the MTDC with sufficient funds to continue to operate and make investments in FY89 and 90.

The MTDC board approved the proposal. Secretary Keefe accepted it and filed the appropriate legislation. "On June 29, 1988 the Corporation made a distribution to the Commonwealth of $750,000. On July 16, 1988, the Legislature and the Governor enacted legislation to accept the distribution … in full satisfaction of all obligations of appropriated funds since inception."[20] While the MTDC would continue to be an integral part of the Commonwealth, it no longer had the obligation to repay these funds.

When I delivered the check for $750,000 to Secretary Keefe's office on June 30, 1988, I was given a warm welcome from him and his executive staff, who were meeting to review the closing of the FY88 books. The MTDC's modest distribution seemed a symbolic gesture demonstrating that the Commonwealth's economic future would be tied to the success of its high-technology sector.

The Economic Climate Changes

The presidential election of 1988 touched MTDC in a small way. During the primary season, MTDC had visitors from several states, including Iowa, who wanted to learn how the Massachusetts economy had become an apparent success. In May 1988, *Fortune* magazine published an article entitled "The Duke: Miracle or Mirage?" in which there was a quote from the founder of Interleaf mentioning the role the

MTDC played in launching the company. However, the article also noted that there was a Massachusetts budget deficit looming in FY88 and Governor Dukakis had cut $233 million in spending for that year.[21]

By the summer of 1988, Governor Dukakis was the presidential nominee of the Democratic Party, but he went on to lose the election in the fall. There were many factors that contributed to his defeat, but the Massachusetts budget shortfall was not the major issue in the campaign. However, a national economic recession was on the horizon. Massachusetts's budget deficits would become a major problem during Governor Dukakis's last two years in office.

In early August 1988, I joined a trade mission to London at the urging of the secretary of economic affairs, Joe Alviani. The main purpose was to meet with financial firms to persuade them to become interested in funding emerging Massachusetts biotechnology companies. While MTDC had not invested in this sector, Secretary Alviani felt it was important to have the Commonwealth's venture capital firm as part of the delegation.

After meeting with venture capitalists, scientists, and British officials, I concluded that MTDC should not consider investing in start-up biotechnology firms. The amount of capital required to finance these firms far exceeded the MTDC's resources and charter limitations. Furthermore, biotechnology investing required specialized scientific knowledge that would be difficult for the MTDC to obtain. This insight was important as we began to develop the MTDC long-range plan.

While the governor's campaign was in progress, New England was just beginning to feel the effects of the national savings-and-loan financial crisis. Bank failures due to speculative real estate loans and fraud had grown from 262 in 1987 to 470 in 1988. They would peak at 534 in

1989. It would not be until 1991 that the Bank of New England failed, but the early signs of a credit crunch were apparent in the region.

The MTDC portfolio companies would need additional dollars to finance their growth because they were not going to be able to obtain loans from banks. This meant that MTDC and its coinvestors would need to reserve more funds for follow-on investment and cut back on the number of start-ups we could launch.

Planning to Go It Alone

Settling the liability to repay the Commonwealth drained $750,000 from the investment fund. The $6.2 million in the treasury in May 1988 had dropped to about $4.8 million by the end of the summer of 1988 after making the payment to the state and closing additional investments. More importantly, MTDC was on notice that it could not expect any additional funding from appropriations for the foreseeable future. Any long-range plan had to involve a strategy to raise more investment capital.

The successful investment harvests in the 1980s had demonstrated that MTDC could become financially self-sufficient. The internal rate of return from the first investment in December 1979 through June 30, 1988, was about 19 percent. There were also a number of companies in the portfolio that looked very promising. For example, 1983 investments in ten companies would eventually yield 4.7 times their cost, for realized gains of over $10.9 million.

- A 1984 investment in Aseco would eventually yield 3.4 times its cost;
- a 1985 investment in Zoom Telephonics returned 9.8 times;
- a 1986 investment in Microtouch returned 4.4 times;
- a 1987 investment in Multilink returned 7.3 times; and

- 1988 investments in IVS and Voicetek returned 2.5 times and 4. 3 times, respectively.

These six investments alone would result in over $13.4 million in realized gains. The total realized gains of over $24 million from all of these 1983 to 1988 investments were 4.6 times the $5.2 million of investment capital that MTDC had received from the Commonwealth.

On the other hand, Massachusetts was about to enter a major economic recession. The following quote from a 1991 report by Prof. Karl E. Case, prepared for the Boston Federal Reserve Bank, summarized the situation.

> The economy of Massachusetts is in a deep recession. In March 1991, the unemployment rate hit 9.7 percent, the second highest in the United States and the worst since 1975. Between the peak of the employment cycle at the end of 1988 and March 1991, the Commonwealth of Massachusetts lost 273,000 jobs, or 8.7 percent of the employment base. By that measure, this recession is much worse than either the 1981–82 recession or the 1975 recession.[22]

Between the credit crunch, the shift by venture capital firms from start-up to follow-on investments, and the lack of liquidity from IPOs for angel investors, new technology enterprises were experiencing great difficulty raising capital. This presented MTDC with a great opportunity to help fill the capital gap. The creation of these new companies would lead to new jobs at these firms and among their suppliers, helping to stimulate the Massachusetts economy.

The MTDC board and staff decided that it would not be wise to pull back from investing in new firms, but we would need to reserve more funds for follow-on investments. The operating plan for FY89 set a goal of $1.8 million of MTDC fund investments in four new companies and additional investments in nine portfolio companies. Also, it targeted $850,000 for three investments from the PRIT fund.

During the fall of 1988, the MTDC board and staff began to develop its long-range plan. Among the questions to be addressed were the following.

1. Should MTDC add to its basic objectives the goal of realizing high rates of return? (The enabling law only required the reasonable prospect of the return on capital invested.)
2. Should we emphasize investment in companies applying established technologies or developing new technology?
3. Should the higher end of the typical investment limit be increased to the statutory level of $500,000? (The average investments through 1986 had not exceeded $360,000.)
4. What role should MTDC play in follow-on investments in portfolio companies?
5. How do we balance the focus on early-stage technology companies with the need to address areas of the Commonwealth such as the west and southeast, where there are fewer of these types of firms?
6. How is the management of funds on behalf of the Massachusetts Pension Reserve Investment Trust (PRIT) as a venture capital firm balanced with MTDC's role as an economic-development agency?
7. What are the implications for MTDC in terms of potential coinvestors as a consequence of the shift of emphasis by venture capital firms toward leveraged buyouts, undervalued public companies, fast-growth service start-ups, and later-stage technology companies?
8. What are the implications for MTDC from the increased investment by foreign corporations in US early-stage technology companies?

9. How does the investment approval process help or hurt? Have we reached the upper limit of new investment with only a maximum of two for each board meeting?
10. Are the investment criteria too complex?
11. Should MTDC staff take board seats with portfolio companies?
12. Given limited resources, should the management-assistance program criteria be tightened?
13. If the staff size remains constant, will the number of portfolio companies per staff member become unreasonably high?
14. Should some investments be merged or liquidated to reduce the number in the portfolio?
15. How can MTDC continue to retain senior professionals? Do we need to reexamine the performance-based compensation plan?

At this point the question of how we would raise additional investment capital had not yet been determined, but it would come to be a major issue in 1989.

Signs of Dark Days Ahead

The one-hundredth regular meeting of the MTDC board of directors was held on January 25, 1989. Howard Smith, chairman, Joe Iandiorio, treasurer, and Tim McNeill were the only remaining private-sector members who were in place when I joined in 1984. Since then, Governor Dukakis had appointed Horace Furumoto, Mary Makela, Ron Payne, Phyllis Swersky, and David Wormley as private-sector members. The secretary of administration and finance, the secretary of economic affairs, and the governor's director of economic development were the three ex officio members, who were represented by their respective designees.

In December 1988, the state auditor's office issued its report on the audit of the MTDC and noted that the past liability of MTDC to repay the Commonwealth had been discharged by the payment of $750,000, but they questioned whether this was in the best interest of the taxpayers. The budget deficit in FY89 was growing, and the auditor's note was a sign of trouble ahead. Public attention was focused on reducing expenses and obtaining revenues for the Commonwealth's general fund. There did not appear to be any interest in supporting programs like the MTDC's, which were designed to create new jobs and help to stimulate the economy. This was especially ironic since MTDC no longer needed state monies to conduct its mission.

Establishing the Plan

In April 1989, the board meeting included a discussion of the long-range plan. We revisited the four key objectives of the MTDC, namely

1. to help create primary employment in technology-based industries in Massachusetts;
2. to attract and leverage private investment in Massachusetts companies;
3. to foster the application of technological innovations where Massachusetts companies are, or can be, leaders; and
4. to nurture entrepreneurship among Massachusetts citizens, planting the seeds for long-term economic development in the Commonwealth.

The accomplishment of these objectives was measured as follows:

1. From 1978 to April 1989, MTDC had invested over $11.9 million and leveraged over $49.7 million of private coinvestment.
2. Forty-nine early-stage technology companies had received investments, and forty-one were currently in active operation.
3. The active companies employed over 3,400 people, with an aggregate annual payroll of over $129 million. It was estimated

that the annual payroll-related taxes to the federal government were $38 million, and to the Commonwealth they were $6 million.

4. Management assistance had been provided to over 385 companies by critiquing business plans and referral to private sources of investment capital.
5. MTDC portfolio companies innovated in the application of technology in areas such as computer-assisted publishing; advanced laser trimming and repair; computer modeling in the petrochemical industry; synthetic crystal production; and software applications for financial research and analysis, import/export management, and manufacturing-requirements planning.

We also reviewed the economic environment and the opportunities ahead. Since World War II, Massachusetts technology companies had been both “pioneers” and “early settlers” that developed innovative products to address problems in several markets. For example, there were several distinct phases during which these companies focused on these opportunities. A few of the markets and some of the iconic leading Massachusetts companies are listed below.

Major New Markets for Technology Products:	Starting Time Frame
1. Aerospace defense (Raytheon)	1940s
2. Scientific and engineering computing (DEC)	1960s
3. Semiconductor manufacturing automation (Teradyne)	1960s
4. Office automation—word processing (Wang)	1970s
5. Applications software (Cullinet)	1970s
6. Health-care information systems (Meditech)	1970s
7. Desktop editing and publishing (Interleaf)	1980s
8. Biotechnology (Genzyme)	1980s
9. Environmental protection (Clean Harbors)	1980s

All of these markets needed technological problem solving. Many new companies were being formed to provide solutions. In addition, as industries began to mature, early leading companies spawned new start-ups. For example, from the minicomputer pioneers such as DEC, Prime Computer, and Data General, many alumni started a wide array of new enterprises.

By the late 1980s, other states and regions had begun to support the commercialization of inventions and innovations, as well as the development of new technology enterprises. For example, the following initiatives had been allocated millions of state dollars:

- the Michigan Strategic Fund—$43 million
- the New Jersey Commission on Science and Technology—$24 million
- the Pennsylvania Ben Franklin Partnership—$32 million
- the Ohio Thomas Edison Program—$16 million
- the New York Science and Technology Foundation—$24 million

In contrast, in Massachusetts, the appropriations totaled $6.5 million for the Centers of Excellence Corporation.

By the end of the 1980s, the Federal Small Business Innovation Research Program (SBIR) created in 1982 had provided grants to hundreds of smaller Massachusetts firms to develop working prototypes of innovative products. Many of these companies were seeking funding to commercialize these products and became management-assistance cases or potential investment prospects of the MTDC.

Given the need for investment capital among early-stage technology entrepreneurs and the proven track record of the MTDC, the board decided that we should proceed ahead with the following plan for the next three years.

- FY90: Invest $1.25 million in four new and up to four portfolio companies
- FY91: Invest $1.15 million in four new and up to two portfolio companies
- FY92: Invest $1.1 million in four new and up to two portfolio companies

This investment plan was based on the assumption of no additional funding from the Commonwealth and a conservative estimate of future harvests.

By the summer of 1989, we thought the MTDC was poised to be a helpful player on the Commonwealth's economic-development team during these challenging times. It turned out that others had a different view of what should happen.

CHAPTER 4

NEGOTIATING A NEW ROLE

Over the late 1989 to 1991 time period, we would face a new series of challenges and opportunities. We knew that a new governor would take office in 1991 and that transition could be potentially disruptive to our plans. However, the legislative proposals to take funds from the MTDC were unexpected. In addition, the emerging national banking crisis would add a new layer of risk assessment. The early 1990s would also see a major shift from investing in computer hardware companies to software firms. We would need to be creative and take the initiative to address these challenges.

Raids on the Treasury

The first sign that the MTDC treasury was a target for other state entities came when the Senate Ways and Means Committee inserted a special provision in its version of the FY90 budget. The language would require the MTDC to provide $195,000 to the Massachusetts Product Development Corporation (MPDC). This was a quasi-public corporation that had been created in the mid-1980s to provide investments to established companies to fund new product development. The returns on these investments would come from royalties on the sales of the products. Generally the companies receiving MPDC funds were more traditional, nontechnology businesses.

When the budget deficits emerged in 1988 and 1989, MPDC's appropriations came under scrutiny. The Senate Ways and Means Committee decided that rather than to once again appropriate funds for the MPDC, it would have MTDC underwrite the FY90 operating expenses.

Instead of simply writing a check to the MPDC, we recommended that the MTDC consider making an investment in that entity. We would then become involved with its board of directors in its oversight. Also, there might be potential returns from this investment if some of MPDC's portfolio companies were successful. This approach would also blunt the setting of a precedent whereby the MTDC's treasury would be raided periodically to fund some other state program. Our recommendation was accepted, and later in the year, the MTDC board approved this investment.

In November 1989, the House Ways and Means Committee reported out the FY90 supplemental budget, which included a section requiring the MTDC to pay not less than $1 million to the general fund by June 30, 1990. This mandatory distribution would have a significant negative impact on the MTDC's ability to fund new and current portfolio companies. In addition, it would have set a bad precedent. Massachusetts was in the middle of a severe recession, when it was critical to launch new enterprises that would create jobs. To reallocate these funds to the general fund would not have made any noticeable dent in the budget deficit. On the other hand, the funds were essential to help start new companies and reverse the economic downturn.

On December 20, 1989, I sent a letter to Secretary of Administration and Finance Lashman to make MTDC's case for the governor to veto this section of the FY90 supplemental budget. At the January 24, 1990, meeting of the MTDC board of directors, I was very happy to report that the governor did veto this provision.

These episodes made it clear that MTDC needed to take the initiative and propose a new model for acquiring investment funds.

Concept of the MTDC Commonwealth Fund

By September 1989, we had developed the concept of a new investment fund that would be comprised of money that MTDC had earned through investment of some of its capital gains, and money from a major investment partner, such as the Massachusetts Pension Fund, PRIT. The initial idea was that MTDC would commit $2,000,000 and PRIT would add $8,000,000. The legal structure would be an investment management agreement lasting ten years, similar to the one we had negotiated with PRIT in 1986. It would be called the MTDC Commonwealth Fund.

The investments from the Commonwealth Fund would focus on second or later-stage rounds of financing in companies that MTDC had helped to launch with money from its traditional fund. The major difference would be that in these later rounds, the companies would not need to demonstrate they were having difficulty raising capital. On the contrary, the expectation was that these investment opportunities would be very attractive to professional coinvestors. The objective of this fund would be to earn a high rate of return. However, it would indirectly aid economic development since all the companies in which it invested would be in Massachusetts. Creating the MTDC Commonwealth Fund would require an amendment to the MTDC enabling act.

The MTDC Commonwealth Fund would limit investment in any one company to $1,000,000, 10 percent of the total committed to the fund. The target initial investment per company would be $500,000. This would enable MTDC to invest in fifteen to twenty companies over the ten-year life of the fund.

The unusual feature of this proposed fund would be that 20 percent of the net gains earned from MTDC's portion of committed capital would be paid to PRIT. The rationale for this approach was that MTDC would distribute a portion of its net gains to an important entity of the Commonwealth, which was already receiving general appropriations to help address the unfunded pension liability. In addition, we thought this would provide an incentive for the management of PRIT to agree to participate in the fund. We also felt that it would be helpful to have the PRIT governing board support our proposed charter amendment in the legislature. They were much more influential with that branch of the government than the MTDC board.

On November 6, 1989, I sent a letter to then-Secretary of Administration and Finance Edward Lashman, in which I summarized the concept of the MTDC Commonwealth Fund described above. I asked for his assistance in filing the appropriate legislation to amend the MTDC charter and notified him that I had begun to discuss this proposal with the PRIT management.

The notion that MTDC would share a portion of its net gains with PRIT was so unusual that the PRIT managers did not seem to appreciate the offer. Instead, they focused on how much they would be asked to commit to the proposed fund. It became clear that this would not be a fruitful partnership. Therefore, we decided to change our approach and have the MTDC 20 percent of net gains go to the Massachusetts general fund. In addition, we decided to seek other investment partners besides PRIT.

On January 15, 1990, Governor Dukakis announced his administration's plan called "Winning in the Nineties: An Economic Strategy for Massachusetts." In the document was the following statement:

> The Governor is sponsoring legislation to set up a new "Commonwealth Fund" at MTDC. Through this new program, MTDC will use a portion of its assets to seed an investment fund whose public and private co-investors would include the state pension fund.[23]

The indifference on the part of the PRIT management made it even more imperative that MTDC move forward with the creation of the MTDC Commonwealth Fund. While the support of the governor was critical, we would need to gain support in the legislature. In July 1990, I reported to the board that Senator Paul White had introduced an outside section of the FY91 budget that would authorize the MTDC Commonwealth Fund.

Governor Dukakis would leave office at the end of 1990, and Governor Weld, a Republican, took over in 1991. The change in administrations and the challenges in dealing with the budget shortfall would require the attention of the Commonwealth's political leaders. It would take another three years before the MTDC Commonwealth Fund amendment would be enacted.

Banking Crisis

The savings-and-loan financial crisis had spread across the nation in 1989. By that year over half the savings and loan banks had failed. Of these failures, half were in the state of Texas. Most of these troubled loans were granted to speculative real-estate and commercial enterprises. It was as if these banks were engaging in high-risk venture capital investing with depositors' money, usually invested in low-risk vehicles like certificates of deposit.

In 1989 Congress created the Resolution Trust Corporation (RTC) to take over and sell troubled assets held by failed banks. Within a few years, this institution would become very well-known in Massachusetts.

For many years, the Bank of New England (BNE) had played a prominent role in lending to commercial enterprises in Massachusetts. Its High-Technology Lending Group had provided loans to many venture capital–backed companies. However, by 1989, the BNE had made speculative real-estate and commercial loans that began to default. That year its board of directors replaced its CEO, and the bank became subject to a federal "cease and desist order" to restrain its lending practices in order to avoid insolvency.[24]

The size and prominence of the BNE's troubled loans and the scrutiny of both federal and Massachusetts bank regulators created an environment in which credit to smaller, emerging companies would be constrained. At the same time, venture capital funding of start-ups was also deceasing. This development was cited in a *Wall Street Journal* article on December 28, 1989, by Udayan Gupta that was headlined, "For Start-ups, Funding Squeeze Tightens."[25]

The weaknesses in the banking system caused the MTDC to be concerned about where to deposit our cash reserves until they were needed to fund investments and operations. Historically, we placed these funds among Massachusetts financial institutions that were viewed as strong and were paying high rates of interest. For example, in the spring of 1990, certificates of deposit of MTDC funds were paying between 7.1 percent and 8.7 percent. The Massachusetts Municipal Deposit Trust at Fidelity investments, which was the major depository for state and local governmental short-term cash reserves, was paying about 8 percent.

Since the Federal Deposit Insurance Corporation only insured accounts of up to $100,000, we had to spread the cash reserves among a number of banks in amounts that did not exceed that limit. In fact, in March

1990, we received a letter from the executive vice president of the BNE thanking us for purchasing a CD of $100,000 as an indication of support for this institution. Of course, this amount was fully insured by the FDIC, and the CD was paying a market interest rate.

The MTDC was now faced with increased demand for investments among start-ups, follow-on financing for portfolio companies dealing with the credit crunch, and risk assessments related to where we placed our cash reserves. In addition, we were planning for a transition in leadership in the governor's administration. It would be a challenging time for the MTDC to take on a new role.

Gubernatorial Transition

The candidates for governor in 1990 were William Weld (Republican) and John Silber (Democrat). On October 23, 1990, a few weeks before the election, the secretary of economic affairs, Alden Raine, sent letters to all of the agencies he supervised asking for transition papers. This was consistent with the professional approach of the Dukakis administration that I had seen in 1978, when Michael Dukakis lost the nomination by the Democratic Party for the governorship to Edward King.

On October 29, 1990, I sent the MTDC transition paper to the secretary. I knew this document would become part of the material given to the next governor's transition team, so it was important to document the accomplishments of the corporation and the composition of its board and staff. Among the information, I included the following.

> By the fall of 1990, the MTDC has made cumulative investments of $15 million in fifty-one companies. It has realized total gains of $6.3 million and losses of $2.2 million, for net gains of $4.1 million. The total capital available for the traditional investment fund has

come from the following sources: Federal $3 million; Commonwealth $5.2 million, and realized gains $4.5 million. In addition, there were $2 million from the Massachusetts Pension Reserve Investment Trust for follow-on investments.

In terms of economic development, there were thirty-nine active firms in which MTDC invested, which had a combined employment of over 4,400. The estimated annual payroll from these jobs was $162 million. The annual payroll-related taxes to the federal government were over $46 million, and $8 million to the Commonwealth.

The MTDC has coinvested with over fifty different venture capital firms, as well as corporate and individual investors. The combined investments from all these sources in the MTDC portfolio companies were over $200 million. The ratio of private coinvestor dollars to MTDC dollars was 13.3 to 1.

The negative impacts of state budget cuts on MTDC were offset by the realized gains. However, it was clear that we could not expect any additional investment capital or operating funds from the state for the foreseeable future. We would need to find other sources. The proposed MTDC Commonwealth Fund would be our vehicle to help access these sources.

The board members in the fall of 1990, and the respective year in which they were first appointed by a governor, were

- Dr. Horace Furumoto, founder and president of Candela Laser—1988;
- Joseph Iandiorio, Esq., intellectual property attorney—1980;

- Benjamin Kincannon, management consultant and former deputy director of the governor's office of economic development—1989;
- Mary Makela, marketing and sales executive—1987;
- Timothy McNeill, president of Wisdom Publishing—1984;
- Howard Smith, chairman, 1983–1990, retired president of Kurzweil Computer Products, and former secretary of economic affairs—1983;
- Phyllis Swersky, executive VP of AICorp—1984; and
- Professor David Wormley, chairman 1990, head of the mechanical engineering department, MIT—1985.

The ex officio members of the board were the secretary of administration and finance, the secretary of economic affairs, and an officer of the Commonwealth designated by the governor.

The staff totaled ten: six professionals and four support personnel.

Since the new governor would have to assemble his own executive team, it would be several months before the leadership of the new administration would be introduced to the MTDC. Our charge was to continue on with the mission as outlined in our long-range plan. We made the point that the MTDC was one of the Commonwealth's economic-development agencies that could help the new administration revive the economy.

Software Trumps Hardware

During the 1980s, many of the companies in which MTDC invested were based on hardware technology. These firms, the year in which they joined the portfolio, and their products were as follows:

- DISCOM (1980—computer screens)
- Xylogics (1980—disk controllers)

- CGX (1982—high-speed workstations)
- Sky Computers (1982—special-purpose computers)
- Proconics (1982—wafer-handling systems)
- Aseco (1984—semiconductor chip-handling systems)
- Zoom (1985—external modems)
- IVS (1988—printed circuit systems)

The products of these companies represented some of the building blocks of the computer-hardware infrastructure.

Software companies added to the portfolio during the 1980s focused on special applications, such as

- Aspen (1981—computer-based modeling and design systems for the petrochemical industry);
- Interleaf (1982—composition and editing systems for diverse content publishers);
- Business Research (1983—computer-based access to investment research);
- Access Technology (1983—spreadsheet software for minicomputers); and
- Aeonic Systems (1984—computer-control systems for sheet-manufacturing companies).

These companies served vertical markets where the entrepreneurs' software expertise had to be tailored to the specialized needs of their target clients. Generally, their software was written to run on the dominant minicomputers of that period, such as IBM, Digital Equipment Corporation (DEC), Hewlett Packard, Data General, and Sun Microsystems.

By the beginning of the 1990s, software companies began to emerge as a preferred investment target for venture capital firms. The gross profit margins for these types of companies were very high. They did not need large amounts of capital to build and equip manufacturing facilities. The number and variety of market niches that they addressed was enormous. The critical talent needed included software designers and programmers, and Massachusetts had a good supply of these specialists.

As 1991 began, the MTDC investment portfolio included several companies that would emerge as financial successes over the next few years. Among these were the following:

- Microtouch, added in 1986. It developed touch screens for specialized applications, and forecasted growing from $12.9 million in 1990 revenue to $16 million in 1991. In 1993 3M acquired this company, and the MTDC realized a multiple of 4.4 times its investment.
- Multilink, added in 1987. It developed and sold teleconferencing systems, and projected growing from $4.6 million in 1990 to $7.5 million in 1991. After it was sold to PictureTel in 2000, MTDC's return was 7.3 times its investment.

The most significant success was Powersoft, a firm that joined the MTDC portfolio in 1983 as Computer Solutions. This company was especially noteworthy because over its life, it built systems on three different computer platforms.

Computer Solutions began with material-requirements planning (MRP) software for smaller manufacturing companies. The software solution was provided through a time-shared computer system, an early version of what we now know as "cloud computing." When MTDC invested in 1983, the company had migrated its software to run on Hewlett Packard minicomputers. In July 1990, the company changed its name to Powersoft in order to reflect its new product, Powerbuilder, client server applications development software on which the company was creating a new MRP System. In early 1991, the company was projecting annual revenue to grow from $17.8 million to $21.8 in the next year.

Later in 1991, the company raised $2.5 million in order to finance its growth plans. The MTDC declined to participate in this round because two well-regarded venture capital firms, Burr Egan & Deleage and Hummer Winblad, decided to become new investors and wanted to invest the entire amount. By this time, the MTDC had been an investor in the company for about eight years. We were reaching the point where an exit would be timely. In fact, in the fall of 1991, the board approved a sale of the MTDC stock to some of the other investors. However, they were unwilling to purchase the shares at the price that we set.

When it became clear that Powerbuilder was perceived as a "hot new" tool for client server applications developers, the company decided to sell off its MRP product line and concentrate on becoming a client server software tool provider. The decision paid off handsomely when the company had an initial public offering in 1993. MTDC then realized a return that was 23.8 times its investment.

Technology Transfer

While waiting for the harvests from these investments, there were other priorities of the new administration that the MTDC had to address. One of these arose because the new economic affairs secretariat under Governor Weld was very interested in the opportunity to commercialize technologies developed in federal laboratories.

The Bayh-Dole Act of 1980 began the revolution allowing technology financed by the federal government in universities to be commercialized. Later there were other laws that reformed how technology would be transferred from federal laboratories. The Stevenson-Wydler Technology Act of 1980 required these laboratories to have a formal technology-transfer program and seek opportunities to partner with industry and universities, as well as state and local government, to move inventions from the labs into real-world applications.

The Technology Transfer Act of 1986 went further and made technology transfer a responsibility of every federal laboratory scientist and engineer. The National Competitiveness Technology Transfer Act of 1989 amended the Stevenson-Wydler Act and made technology transfer the mission of government-owned and contractor-operated laboratories and their employees. It also clarified the manner in which Cooperative Research and Development Agreements (CRADAs) would be implemented. The CRADAs became a major vehicle through which technology transfers would take place.

Additional incentives for technology transfer came from Executive Order 12591 in 1987, which spelled out revenue-sharing programs with inventors employed by the federal labs, and defined cash awards programs. The laboratories themselves would also benefit from these programs both directly and by encouraging key scientists and engineers to continue as employees. By 1990 federal laboratories became proactive in trying to inform potential partners about technology-transfer opportunities. The department of defense laboratories in Massachusetts were especially aggressive.

In May 1990, a Technology Transfer Forum was held at Middlesex Community College. The MTDC and other state agencies cosponsored this forum with the US Air Force Electronic Systems Commander, General Fornell, of Hanscom Air Force Base. He was also the head of the Massachusetts Military Coalition. Representatives of the laboratories displayed samples of their research to more than 150 attendees at the forum and explained the potential for CRADAs.

In May 1991, the Second Annual Technology Transfer Forum was held at the Worcester Polytechnic Institute. The new governor, William Weld, spoke at this event and underscored his support for this activity. The secretary of economic affairs, Dan Gregory, was also interested in technology transfer. That summer a member of Secretary Gregory's staff and I spent many hours advising some entrepreneurs who were planning to apply to the federal government to establish a regional technology-transfer center in Massachusetts.

The product-development grants from the Small Business Innovation Research (SBIR) program launched by Congress in 1982 and the technology-transfer opportunities emerging from the federal laboratories would become very interesting to technology-oriented entrepreneurs. We made it a point to advise both our portfolio companies and others to explore these programs.

Defining the Purposes of the MTDC

With a new governor and his administration in office, it became important for the MTDC to more explicitly define its purposes. Most of the new public officials were not familiar with the MTDC's operations and track record. If we wanted to map our own future, we needed to take the initiative.

When the original enabling act creating the MTDC was signed into law in 1978, the basic purpose of the corporation was somewhat vaguely stated. In section 3 of Chapter 40G of the Massachusetts General Laws (MGL) was the following provision:

> The MTDC shall have all of the powers necessary to carry out its purposes which shall include but not be limited to …[26]

This was followed by a long list of typical corporate ministerial powers.

In section 8, there was the following provision, which was generally designed to guide a court's interpretation of the statute:

> This Chapter shall be liberally construed to effect its purposes.[27]

For thirteen years the board of directors had duly authorized the policies and operations of the MTDC without specifically defining its purposes. The statute was so specific in its definition of terms and investment policy limitations that the purposes seemed to be obvious. However, with the inauguration of a new governor, the board felt it was timely to spell out the MTDC's purposes.

At the February 27, 1991, board meeting, the following resolution was adopted:

> Pursuant to its enabling statute, specifically Chapter 40G Section 2, The corporation shall be governed and its corporate power exercised by a board of directors which shall consist of eleven directors … The Board of Directors hereby resolves:
>
> That the purposes of the MTDC include but are not limited to: (i) helping to create primary employment in technology based enterprises in the Commonwealth, (ii) fostering the development of such enterprises in the Commonwealth through the purchase of qualified securities to provide seed capital, (iii) attracting and managing the investment of both public and private funds in such enterprises, and (iv) nurturing entrepreneurship among the citizens of the Commonwealth to stimulate long-term economic development.[28]

Among the board members voting to approve this resolution were the designees of the two ex officio members appointed by Governor Weld. Secretary Peter Nessen of administration and finance (A & F) had designated James Hearty, and Secretary Dan Gregory of economic affairs (EA) had assigned Dan Daly. Both of these designees had business experience and appreciated the role that the MTDC would play in helping the new administration address the economic-development challenges facing the Commonwealth.

Legislation to Create the Commonwealth Fund

It was especially helpful to have the MTDC's purposes defined as we prepared for the upcoming legislative hearing on the bill that would authorize the MTDC to create the Commonwealth Fund. Senate bill 92 was scheduled to be presented to the joint commerce and labor committee on March 6, 1991.

The objectives of the proposed Commonwealth Fund were

1. to focus early-stage patient investment capital on innovative technology-based companies;
2. to encourage the start-up and expansion of companies with high value-added products that address newer market opportunities outside of Massachusetts and add to its export base; and
3. to provide direct attractive financial returns to investors and indirect economic benefits to the Commonwealth in the form of new jobs, purchases of goods and services in the local economy, and tax revenues.

The legislation would authorize the MTDC to allocate a portion of its assets to create the Commonwealth Fund and seek coinvestors in the fund who would contract with the MTDC for its management. The goal was for the MTDC to allocate $1 million and secure $4 to $9 million of coinvestment. These funds would then be invested in twelve to eighteen companies over a three- to six-year period in amounts ranging from $300,000 to $800,000.

At the hearing on March 6, 1991, Bob Crowley and I testified about the plan and operations of the Commonwealth Fund. In addition, several past private-sector coinvestors joined in support of the bill. These included Tom Claflin of Claflin Capital Management, Wade Blackmun of American Research and Development, and Paul Kelly of Zero Stage Capital. Letters of support were also submitted by the following MTDC portfolio-company executives: Mark Ain of Kronos, Brian Crowley of Graftel, Jim Hayes of Fotec, Mitchell Kertzman of Powersoft, Frank Manning of Zoom Telephonic, Ed McAteer of Multilink, Jack Rennie of Pacer Systems, and Jack Wolf of Tytronics.

Professionals who had collaborated with the MTDC also submitted their support for the bill. These included John Ciccarelli of the UMASS Small Business Development Center; Paul Johnson of the MIT Enterprise Forum; Ronald Maheu of Coopers and Lybrand; Marijo McCarthy of Widett, Glazer, and McCarthy; Judy Obermayer of the MIT Enterprise Forum; Joyce Plotkin of the Massachusetts Software Council; and Ken Smith of the Massachusetts Business Development Corporation.

The bill would be deliberated within the joint committee on commerce and labor. It would be several months before any action would be taken on the proposal.

CHAPTER 5

VENTURE INVESTING CHALLENGES

Capital and Credit Shortages

While the MTDC remained financially sound during the 1990–1991 recession, the venture capital investing and bank credit climate had changed. The savings-and-loan crisis had a major impact on bank business lending. Banks were required to reduce their loan portfolios. In many instances, this meant that they would call in loans from some of their successful customers. Most venture capital firms had to allocate more money to fund their current portfolio companies versus launch new enterprises.

The Venture Capital Journal included an article in its June 1991 edition entitled "Venture Capital Disbursements Declined 43% to $2 Billion in 1990." It reported that "seed financings fell 57% from $138 million in 1989 to $60 million in 1990." These represented national data. The key regional changes were that California was down 41 percent and Massachusetts was down 35 percent.[29]

In May 1991, the Small Business Administration announced an "innovative revolving credit program" in the depressed New England states and projected the demand for these loans to be $16 to $20 million.[30]

These developments underscored the need for capital and credit that was dampening the economic recovery in Massachusetts. Companies had to find unusual sources of capital, and the MTDC saw a steady flow of new investment prospects.

During FY90 and FY91, the total available cash in the MTDC treasury ranged between $3.5 and $4 million. These funds were allocated to support the current portfolio, as well as underwrite operations, which left relatively little for new investments. Our potential coinvestors were generally in a similar financial position, making it difficult to pull deals together. The pressure to find new sources of investment capital was intensifying, and we began to explore a variety of alternatives.

Potential Sources of Capital

While the Commonwealth Fund legislation was still under consideration, we began to look at sources of capital that might fit within the existing charter of the MTDC or could fit within the proposed Commonwealth Fund.

On August 6, 1991, I testified before the governor's Special Commission on Financial Services. This commission was established to address the capital-and-credit crunch. One of the ideas the commission was considering was a Massachusetts Development Bank, which would pool investors, particularly those from the Pacific Rim, who would be interested in potential returns from investing in Massachusetts's innovative companies. Provisions of the 1990 Immigration Act also supported the investment pool concept. This law stipulated that if an employment-creating immigrant investor committed at least $1 million in enterprises adding ten or more jobs, he or she would have an opportunity to become a permanent resident of the United States.

I wrote a letter on August 16, 1991, to the Immigration and Naturalization Service commenting on the proposed regulations, INS N. 1434-91, pertaining to employment-creating immigrant investors. I suggested that the rules include a provision for an employment-creating immigrant to invest in economic-development funds that would help to finance new companies. Our experience at the MTDC led me to estimate that if ten employment-creating immigrants each invested $1 million in a fund that the corporation managed and the MTDC added $1 million from its own assets, we could finance twelve new or expanding technology companies. Of these, I estimated nine might be successful, and from among these companies, 126 to 396 direct jobs would be created.

Unfortunately, neither of the above initiatives ultimately resulted in the creation of new capital pools for young technology companies. We needed to continue our search for new sources of investment dollars.

MTDC Status: Summer 1991

On October 3, 1991, I wrote a memorandum to the board summarizing the FY91 accomplishments and outlining the FY92 plan.

During FY91 we added six new companies to the portfolio: Augment Systems, Endogen, Exos, Reflection Technology, StatSpin Technologies, and Technology Integration Development Group. Three of the six were in the start-up phase: Augment, Exos, and Reflection. The other three were beginning to expand. These six companies represented the largest number of additions to the portfolio in a twelve-month period since the stock market crash of 1987.

While the MTDC did not specifically target industry sectors, the companies in which it had invested were broken down as follows:

- Computer software and services: 11 companies
- Computer equipment and peripherals: 7 companies
- Industrial automation systems and equipment: 9 companies
- Biomedical: 6 companies
- Telecommunications and data communications: 6 companies
- Material science and related systems: 2 companies
- Advanced defense systems and products: 2 companies
- Environmental management: 1 company

By the end of FY91, MTDC had exited twenty-seven of the companies in which it had invested. The following summarizes these results.

- Eight had completed successful public offerings: Cambridge Analytics Associates, DISCOM, Interleaf, Pacer Systems, Spire, Vitronics, Xylogics, and Zoom.
- Ten had been acquired by other firms: Access, Aeonic, Amherst, Business Research Corporation, CGX, Chromatic, Harbor Medical, Randwall, Saum, and Wakefield.
- Two bought back their stock from MTDC: AMDEV and Crystal Systems.
- Finally, seven had ceased operations: Ikier, Practek, Publishing Technology, Solenergy, Spectrovision, Tactics (GSI), and Telphi.

As a result of these exits, the MTDC realized cumulative gains since its inception of $7.3 million and realized losses of $3.1 million, for net realized gains of $4.2 million.

Total investment funds at the end of FY91 came from the following sources: US Department of Commerce EDA $3 million, Commonwealth of Massachusetts $5.2 million, and gains from previous MTDC investments $5 million.

In terms of job creation, as of December 30, 1990, 4,800 people were employed among the forty active companies in which the MTDC had invested. The estimated annual payroll for all of these employees was about $186 million, which generated annual payroll-related taxes to the federal government of $52 million and almost $10 million to the Commonwealth.

Strategic Alternatives

Notwithstanding these accomplishments, there was a compelling need to conserve resources during this period of economic retrenchment. For FY92, the operating budget of the MTDC was reduced by 3 percent. However, it was essential to continue funding new companies, so our investment plan for FY92 was to commit a total of $1.5 million to five new companies and one portfolio company. While this allocation was far below the apparent demand, we decided to maintain our reserves to fund existing portfolio companies during what appeared to be a prolonged economic drought. Fortunately by the middle of FY92, we were able to project $1.5 million more in realized gains than we had planned for the year. We were now able to project that by the end of the fiscal year, we would commit a total of $2.1 million to eight new and twelve current portfolio companies.

When we held our long-range planning meeting in January 1992, the strategic alternatives the board considered were as follows:

> Plan A: Commonwealth Fund Approach: This plan assumed we would be successful in securing $5 to $10 million of new capital for equity investments.
>
> Plan B: Revolving Loan Approach: This plan assumed we would allocate most of the funds for subordinated

debt investments and shift our emphasis from start-up to expansion-stage companies.

The board chose plan A: Commonwealth Fund Approach. The corporation would continue its mission to help launch start-up technology companies. Once again, the Commonwealth Fund bill would be proposed in 1992. This time it was Senate Bill 66, filed by Senator Lois Pines, Senator David Magnani, and Representative Suzanne Bump.

Reorganizing the Quasi-Public Corporations

By the second year of the Weld administration in 1992, most of the budget cutting had been done. Now the primary concern was to stimulate the recovery of the Massachusetts economy. Among the tools the administration had at its disposal were the various quasi-public organizations that had an economic-development mission. While the governor appointed the members of the boards of directors of these organizations, they were independent entities. The administration decided it needed to take greater control of these tools.

On January 17, 1992, the governor issued an executive order creating "An Advisory Committee on the Coordination of the Economic Development Programs of the Commonwealth."[31] The quasi-public organizations that were to be reviewed included

- the MTDC;
- the Massachusetts Industrial Finance Agency (MIFA);
- the Massachusetts Community Development Finance Corporation (CDFC);
- the Massachusetts Government Land Bank;
- the Economic Stabilization Trust (EST);
- the Industrial Services Program (ISP);

- the Massachusetts Product Development Corporation (MPDC);
- Bay State Skills Corporation (BSSC);
- the Massachusetts Technology Park Corporation (MTPC);
- the Massachusetts Health and Education Finance Authority (HEFA);
- the Massachusetts Housing Finance Agency (HFA); and
- the Massachusetts Office of Business Development (MOBD).

These "alphabet soup" organizations had been created over the previous fifteen to twenty years to address specific economic-development challenges. For example, the Government Land Bank was established to deal with the closing of military bases in the Commonwealth. The Bay State Skills Corporation (BSSC) was created to develop and run targeted industry technical skills training where there were acute shortages of qualified workers. The Health and Education Finance Authority (HEFA) provided a mechanism for hospitals, colleges, and universities to finance building construction and renovation. The MTDC, MIFA, and CDFC were all designed to address different types and stages of companies needing capital to start or grow.

It was understandable that the administration would want to reorganize these agencies to better coordinate their services. However, each had been created with governing boards that were designed to be independent of "political manipulation." Each had well-defined and targeted missions, and most had sources of funding that were separate from the annual budget-appropriation process. Furthermore, they had performance track records over several years and stakeholders who had come to rely on their programs.

By the summer of 1992, the advisory committee recommended that the quasi-publics should be reorganized into three "super divisions":

- Business development
- Nonprofit financing
- Distressed-area financing

However, the idea of creating new bureaucracies, the resistance of the various stakeholder groups, and a legislature dominated by the opposite party from the governor all made it unlikely that these recommendations would be adopted.

At the MTDC one of our greatest concerns was the potential loss of very high-caliber volunteers on the board of directors if the organization was consolidated under a large new bureaucracy. These individuals donated their time and expertise because they knew their investment decisions had an impact. Furthermore, the board controlled the staffing and operations of the corporation. The quality of the board members was a major contributor to the success of the MTDC.

In the fall of 1992, it appeared that the reorganization plan was not gaining traction in the legislature. Secretary of Economic Affairs Steve Tocco signaled that he would be willing to consider alternatives to better coordinate the services of the quasi-publics. The legislature agreed to create the "Quasi Public Coordinating Council" (QPCC), which would be comprised of the heads of these organizations and overseen by the Massachusetts Office of Business Development (MOBD) within the economic affairs secretariat. The QPCC ran cross-training programs for all the staff of the various organizations so that they would be better able to refer potential clients to the appropriate agency. In addition, the members of the QPCC jointly funded regional specialists on the staff of MOBD who would also be able to refer clients to any of these agencies.

Now that the MTDC would not be subsumed under a new bureaucracy, we could continue to chart our own course. Raising additional investment capital continued to be our major priority. Among the potential sources we considered were PRIT, the federal SBIC program, and the proposed Massachusetts Agricultural Entrepreneur's Fund. These alternatives are outlined below.

PRIT II

The Pension Reserve Investment Management Trust (PRIT) program the MTDC managed since 1986 was producing positive results. Therefore, we approached the leadership of the Pension Reserve Investment Management (PRIM) board to see if they would be interested in having the corporation manage a second investment program. However, when we explained that the size of the fund would be limited to about $20 million, their response was that they were targeting investing at least $10 million in any venture capital partnerships and they did not want to own more than 10 percent of any fund. Consequently, PRIT would not be a fruitful source for the capital MTDC needed to continue its mission.

SBIC Program

In 1992, Congress passed the Small Business Equity Enhancement Act, Title IV of Public Law 102366. There were several changes to the SBIC program that were interesting to the MTDC. The first was that public pension fund investment could be considered "private capital." The second was an interpretation by the Small Business Agency (SBA) that funds owned by a public instrumentality that were generated from fees, interest income, or gains could be treated as "private capital." And the third was that up to 33 percent of an SBIC's private capital could be in the form of a direct investment by a state or local government, so long as the SBIC was privately managed and the balance of its capital came from purely private sources.

Since the MTDC's enabling legislation included authorization to operate as an SBIC, the new provisions offered a potential legal structure for the corporation in order to secure investment capital from this federal program. The critical issue would be whether the MTDC could create an entity that would be completely privately managed. The experience we had with the administration's efforts to reorganize the MTDC with other quasi-public organizations raised some serious questions about the degree to which the Commonwealth would agree to allow the MTDC to become even more independent. For the time being, this question was put on hold.

Agricultural Entrepreneur's Fund

The Massachusetts Commissioner of Agriculture Greg Watson sent me a letter on October 25, 1992, suggesting that the MTDC might work with his department and other groups, such as the New England Small Farms Institute, to foster the development of innovative food-related businesses. The agriculture department was considering issuing a request for proposal from the MTDC to manage a revolving loan fund that would be targeted at the above-mentioned types of businesses. The initial size of the fund would be about $500,000.

While we did give serious consideration to this concept, the RFP never materialized. In hindsight, it was probably a positive outcome since it might have caused us to be less focused on our core competency of investment in technology enterprises.

Harvesting Gains from the MTDC Portfolio

By December 1992, one of the MTDC's portfolio companies, Powersoft Corporation, was planning on an initial public offering (IPO) in early 1993. On December 9, 1992, I wrote a memorandum to the board indicating that the potential gains from this investment might provide enough funds to cover our basic investment program for the subsequent twelve to eighteen months.

In fact, the gains realized from the Powersoft investment in 1993 totaled about $6.9 million. This was almost as much as had been realized from all investments since MTDC's first in 1979 through the end of FY91. It would also be greater than the cumulative $5.2 million that the Commonwealth had appropriated for the MTDC investment fund between 1980 and 1988.

As we entered 1993, the most reliable source of MTDC's capital was its own investment portfolio. The gains could be redeployed to invest in a new generation of start-up and early-stage technology companies. We did not need to deviate from our strategic mission and chase sources of capital that might have caused us to lose focus.

Venture Investing and Economic Development

In August 1991, the *Venture Capital Journal* published an article titled "Long Dismissed by Venture Capitalists, State Programs Are Gaining Respect." The author, John G. F. Bonnanzio, highlighted that between 1988 and 1990, private firms' investments in seed and start-up companies dropped from $577 million to $202 million. During this same period, state funds grew from $104 million to $269 million. Bonnanzio quoted Professor Richard Meyer, the author of the *Emory Business School Report* titled "The 1991 National Census of Public and Private Seed Capital Funds," as saying, "Public programs have stepped in to fill the gap."[32]

The article went on to describe several of the state funds and the problems associated with investment programs linked to political leadership. For example, the author mentioned that political pressures might lead to unwise investments. In addition, since a state fund may limit its investments to companies within its borders, the quality of the deal flow may not be as robust as needed. However, in Massachusetts, deal flow from high-technology start-ups was not an obstacle due to the concentration of universities, teaching hospitals, research centers, and established high-tech companies within a fifty-mile radius of Boston.

The author then went on to mention the MTDC, writing,

> Despite these problems there are state venture funds that have risen effortlessly above the fracas of partisan politics. Massachusetts is often referred to by fund managers as an example of how a state fund should be run. Founded in 1978, the Massachusetts Technology Development Corporation was created to finance early stage technology companies and to-date has funded 55 of them.[33]

A few years later, the public-policy emphasis shifted to the development of "Economically Targeted Investment (ETI) Programs" managed by state public pension funds. The idea was to allocate a portion of the pension funds to be invested through private managers, who would agree to target investments within the respective state.

In 1995 this approach led to the creation and financing by the Massachusetts public pension funds of a new private venture capital firm called Commonwealth Capital Ventures. This firm continues today to invest in new enterprises, generally located in Massachusetts. The ETI program added other private venture funds as managers in subsequent years.

While the MTDC was the first venture firm to manage an "ETI" fund for PRIT, the new model adopted in the early 1990s prevailed. However, as the size of the private venture limited partnerships grew, the capital gap faced by very early-stage technology firms continued. If a company was trying to raise less than $1 million, was started by a first-time entrepreneur, and was still in the early years of product development and introduction, it would generally have difficulty raising money. The start-ups that were pursuing vertical or niche markets were usually outside the preferred investment focus of the growing private venture capital firms.

National Concern Regarding Seed/Early-Stage Capital

In 1993, there was a bill in Congress titled "The Civilian Technology Venture Capital Act of 1993." The House Committee on Science, Space, and Technology described the purpose of the bill as follows.

> Promote the advancement, maturation, and application of critical and other advanced technology by increasing the amount and reducing the cost of equity capital available and committed to domestic companies …[34]

On January 5, 1993, I wrote a letter to the staff of the Subcommittee on Technology and Competitiveness of the US House Committee on Science, Space, and Technology, which was considering a Critical Technologies Development Bill. I suggested that the bill should address the following goals: (1) realign equity capital for more patient investment, (2) strengthen the network of firms doing seed/early-stage deals, and (3) enable firms to efficiently invest smaller amounts of capital.

These initiatives arose from a growing concern that new technology enterprises were unable to secure investments to launch and grow. This was happening in an environment when after the collapse of the Soviet Union, the US defense budgets, especially R & D, were being reevaluated. The idea was that the country needed to find more effective ways to commercialize the technologies that could be spun out from the Defense R & D activities.

In many ways, the public-policy discussions during this period were very similar to those in the 1970s, when MTDC was being created.

The capital gap facing start-up and early-stage technology companies was continuing to be a challenge.

Applications for Vertical Markets

During the early 1990s, the MTDC portfolio began to include companies that were developing applications for vertical markets. The following companies illustrate a few of these applications.

> In 1990, Reflection Technology produced a tool to visualize computer displays through a tiny screen held in front of one eye. This technology seemed to appeal to companies in the video-game market.
>
> Also in 1990, Exos created an electronic exoskeleton that enabled the control of a robotic hand.
>
> In 1991, AT-Comm was one of the first developers of an automated toll-collection system like what we now know as EZ-Pass.
>
> In 1992, Sensitech produced a sensing and computer recording system that enabled precise measurement of temperatures of refrigerated products in transit.
>
> In 1993, Pixelvision produced one of the earliest versions of flat-screen computer displays.
>
> In 1994, Venturecom provided software tools for embedded computer systems.
>
> In 1995, MicroE developed precision measuring systems for computer disk controllers.

Between 1990 and 1996, the MTDC added thirty new companies to its portfolio. Of these, eleven resulted in positive returns. Two of these produced more than ten times the money invested. However, for most of these companies, it would take five to ten years before an exit strategy took place. In the meantime, these firms employed hundreds of people and purchased goods and services from a broad array of local suppliers.

Three of the additions to the portfolio during this period were Fiberspar, Pixelvision, and SelecTech. Each of these cases illustrates the diversity of the types of companies and market niches they pursued. They represented the robust array of investment opportunities found in the Massachusetts innovation economy. Rob Frohman reported the stories of the entrepreneurs behind these companies as follows.

Peter Quigley—Fiberspar

Peter Quigley is a natural entrepreneur and got his start at a relatively early age. Identifying his business plan while studying at M.I.T., he was intrigued by capitalizing on the manufacture of fiber-reinforced composites. Mr. Quigley founded Fiberspar in 1986 to produce continuous fiber-reinforced composite products for the high-end sports market. At 23 years old, and with little preparation, Mr. Quigley valued the competition and challenge of starting a company. To him it was applied education.

Mr. Quigley had unique insights into manufacturing and while at M.I.T., looked at textile manufacturing as a framework for building fiber-reinforced plastics. This understanding coupled with the insight that athletes will accept and pay for high end equipment, led Mr. Quigley to target the high-end sports market as the place to start with these materials. This was also an area Mr. Quigley had a particular passion for as he had pursued a spot on the US Sailing Team for the 1984 Olympics.

Understanding the value of networks, Mr. Quigley started Fiberspar with several friends, leveraging their networks as well in raising capital. Quickly exhausting the initial seed money and facing challenges early on like Black Monday in October 1987, Mr. Quigley spent his time as a full time fund-raiser. Eventually the work paid off with a 24 hour production facility and a solid distribution channel. The mast business expanded and Fiberspar was able to advertise 10 world sailing champions. Fiberspar was also expanding into the production of hockey sticks. During this period from 1987 to 1991, the business was largely built on loans taken from friends and family. Mr. Quigley appreciates having the flexibility at this time to build the products and methods to achieve his early vision.

In 1991, and looking to expand past sports products, Mr. Quigley investigated the manufacture of spool-able pipe for the oil and gas industry. It was at this time he met with the Massachusetts Capital Resource Company and MTDC, with a way to attract capital without losing control of the business. Mr. Quigley recounted, “As the founder, the pressure is on you to raise capital and ensure that the company has the resources it needs.” In 1996, Fiberspar acquired all the intellectual property from a partnership with Conoco and joined a partnership with Halliburton Energy Services to further develop the spool-able pipe. Fiberspar continues to grow and in the past 8 years has installed more than 50 million feet of pipe by over 450 oil and gas producers.

In 2000, Fiberspar sold the sporting goods division to focus on spool-able pipe. In his experience with MTDC, Mr. Quigley felt there was no difference in dealing with the organization over traditional VC. They were flexible on terms and worked well together. Mr. Quigley takes pride in the Fiberspar exit for MTDC, remarking that perhaps they had gotten out too early.

In 2012 the global oil field product and service company, NOV, acquired Fiberspar. This transaction provided significant returns to the investors.

An initial MTDC investment was made in October 1992 and exited through debt repayment and stock redeemed in September 2002. The capital return rate was 204% with an IRR of 18.3%, per MTDC reports.[35]

Vic Odryna—Pixelvision

Entrepreneurship is "in my DNA, and both of my kids as well." Vic Odryna loves to create things and grew up in a technology environment with both parents working in science and engineering. He received a B.Sc. in Electrical Engineering and a M. Sc. in Computer Science. Mr. Odryna was not driven by wealth, but by the desire to build something of lasting value, a common entrepreneurial value. He enjoys solving problems and being successful in doing it.

Mr. Odryna started his career writing microcode at Digital, and then HP after the acquisition. Frustrated by the focus on "building a better mousetrap," Mr. Odryna felt that reinventing complex systems to build features customers did not want was not what he wanted to do, so joined a technology transition team at HP. In this new role, he gained significant business experience working in mergers and acquisitions.

In 1991, Mr. Odryna partnered with a peer to start a company. Both were frustrated as engineers and wanted to create something new. Working nights and weekends for the first four months they spent time talking and working with business plans, though no solid technology idea came to them. They decided that the approach was not working so quit their jobs and mortgaged their houses to fuel the fire. Learning on the street, Mr. Odryna felt, was the way to go. Academics were too slow. They spent their time thinking about what technology was coming and centered on flat panel displays. At the time, 640x480 density was improving so Mr. Odryna decided to buy 3 Sharp Active Matrix displays. Realizing they could not compete on the underlying technology, they decided to focus on packaging and solutions.

Pixelvision partnered with HP to work with HP Medical and they also looked at financial trading as a potential market. The Pixelvision approach of consolidating data with displays proved effective for the NYSE and Pixelvision started to grow. Year to year, they saw revenues grow from $400k to $2 million, then onto $11 million. Mr. Odryna needed capital but did not have the time to pursue it. It was at this time that

Mr. Odryna was introduced to MTDC who helped Pixelvision develop a business plan through the Blue Book process. Mr. Odryna proudly recounted how Pixelvision was the first in the MTDC portfolio to meet its 4-year projections.

Looking at his experience with MTDC, Mr. Odryna sees MTDC as recognizing their investment is in the person or the team. A top down approach is worthless; it is the bottom-up that counts until you something sells. He recalled Bob Crowley remarking, "Nothing happens until someone sells something." In the end, the investors do not know what the team does; they need to trust the team. Mr. Odryna saw MTDC as playing its role well, somewhere between seed and VC funding, providing an opportunity to build additional capital on that initial investment.

An initial MTDC investment was made in August 1993 and exited through sale of the company in May 2000. The capital return rate was 133% with an IRR of 5.8%, per MTDC reports.[36]

Tom Ricciardelli—SelecTech

Always having a desire to work outside the box and create, Tom Ricciardelli founded SelecTech in 1993 with the mission of "creating valuable products from scrap." Today, SelecTech uses innovative design methods to develop specialized flooring which is up to 60% recycled content and is 100% recyclable.

Mr. Ricciardelli was trained in engineering and business, receiving a B.Sc. in Chemical Engineering and an M.B.A from the M.I.T. Sloan School of Management. After leaving school, Mr. Ricciardelli joined a chemical company but soon after returned to Massachusetts to take a position with a startup company that recycled medical waste. He was hired as a business analyst evaluating unit cost analysis and profitability as the company attempted to commercialize their technology. When the decision to build a factory was made, Mr. Ricciardelli volunteered to do the job, selling himself and getting involved. Unfortunately, the factory did not pay off and the company acquired negative cash flow. As Mr. Ricciardelli recalled, "There is no in-between. They swung a big bat and missed."

At 30 years old, Mr. Ricciardelli felt he had sufficient experience and wanted to start a company of his own. He had practical business having started a factory and had built a good network around recycling. Unintimidated by the prospects, Mr. Ricciardelli wrote a business plan and began the search for capital. His desire was to build value through recycling and was looking for enough capital to build a factory. Only receiving $1 million out of a required $4 million, SelecTech partnered with Dupont to develop industrial floor tile. When the division of Dupont disbanded, it left SelecTech with a good product though very little capital. Mr. Ricciardelli received enough however to focus on the development of product for markets in commercial, ESD, and residential basement flooring.

Leveraging his experience working for the medical recycling company and some time consulting, Mr.

Ricciardelli found raising capital as exciting. It was at this time that Mr. Ricciardelli was introduced to MTDC and John Hodgman. Mr. Ricciardelli felt that MTDC understood the big picture and understood the drivers behind the business he was trying to build. He had a passion for business and wanted to build SelecTech. As well, he felt that VC might find the safest way to build the business would be to replace the technologists with professional managers and it was very important to Mr. Ricciardelli that he retain control.

MTDC invested $250k, though Mr. Ricciardelli had hoped to receive more as he had difficulty raising the additional VC funds. However, he was determined to make it work. It took an additional three years to work through the technical kinks, something that may have come faster with more capital. Today, SelecTech manufactures a variety of flooring products from recycled materials for application in commercial and residential markets.

Mr. Ricciardelli feels that the quasi-public nature of MTDC is more open to supporting ownership and feels a primary motivator behind the people of MTDC is passion and vision.

An initial MTDC investment was made in July 1995 with an exit write off in December 2005, per MTDC reports.[37]

In March 2014, when Tom Ricciardelli reviewed the above write-up, he added:

> I'd add that the MTDC is more open to business creation and risk taking than other forms of venture financing. I have to say (truly) that the vision you engendered at the MTDC of promoting new business creation is extraordinary. We also got great support from the organization, especially when times were difficult.[38]

Companies that focused on niche markets comprised the vast majority of the MTDC portfolio. Overall they provided respectable returns, good singles and doubles. Only Powersoft was a home run up to this time. The thirty-one companies added to the portfolio between 1979 and 1984 received $8.2 million and returned $24.1 million. The eighteen added between 1985 and 1989 received $9.3 million and returned $19.3 million. Finally, the $15.3 million invested in thirty companies between 1990 and 1996 returned $18.8 million. Most of these returns did not take place until five to seven years after the initial investment by the MTDC. However, the employment created by these companies extended over all the years that they were operating.

CHAPTER 6

BEFORE THE INTERNET

In the early to mid-1990s, companies engaged in business-to-business selling, not business-to-consumer, were prevalent among technology-based firms in Massachusetts. They were developing innovative solutions to enable businesses to be more efficient in developing their products and services or improving the way they sold these products. The phenomenon called the Internet was just starting to appear. This new technology platform would change the way products and services would be sold to consumers and to other businesses. It would also enable the creation of social-media enterprises on a scale that was unimaginable.

The following sections provide an overview of the new enterprise environment and the status of the MTDC during the pre-Internet years of the 1990s. It was a time when the patterns of venture capital investing would begin to change in size and industry focus.

While the Cambridge/128 areas were generally thought of as the center of high-technology entrepreneurship, the MTDC had to look more broadly throughout Massachusetts since its charter limited it to investments in the Commonwealth. The deal flow would vary within different regions of the state.

Regional Patterns of Technology Firms

One indicator of where new technology companies were emerging was the pattern of applicants to the MTDC from the Commonwealth's counties. For example, the following illustrates where the companies were located in late 1992.

> Sixty-one percent of the applicants were located in Middlesex County, which included Cambridge and many of the cities and towns along the northwestern arc of the Route 128 beltway.
>
> Next was Essex County on the North Shore, where 13 percent of the applicants originated.
>
> Third was Suffolk County, essentially the city of Boston, with 10 percent.
>
> Norfolk County, encompassing communities to the south of Boston, generated 5 percent.
>
> Plymouth County in the southeastern region and Worcester County in the central region each had 3 percent.
>
> The three counties in the western part of the state—Hampden, Hampshire, and Franklin—each recorded 1 percent.

Universities like MIT and Harvard in Cambridge were very important in spawning new technology enterprises in that city. However, established high-tech companies located along Route 128 were also a major source of new companies. The engineers and scientists who had worked for these firms and decided to leave to start their own businesses usually chose locations within a reasonable commuting distance from their homes.

Efforts were made to create a more favorable environment for technology entrepreneurs near the research centers at the University of Massachusetts in Amherst. However, a critical mass was very slow to develop. The more low-key lifestyle valued in the western region of the state contributed some cultural obstacles. Furthermore, the skilled technology professionals who could be recruited as companies grew were fewer in the west than in the greater Boston area.

On the other hand, the University of Massachusetts at Lowell was a very good source of technology-oriented entrepreneurs and workers. This campus had a long history of providing technological innovations, first in the textile industry and later in plastics. The culture of this Middlesex County region was very much in synch with high tech.

The Worcester region also offered promise. The MTDC decided to support the efforts of the newly established Worcester Polytechnic Institute's Venture Forum. Like the MIT Enterprise Forum, this initiative helped to inspire technology start-ups and facilitated seed investments in many of them. Bob Creeden from the MTDC was an active leader in this initiative.

Public Recognition

While the MTDC operated as transparently as possible, we preferred to publicize the accomplishments of the portfolio companies, rather than the corporation itself. We issued press releases whenever an investment was made. We encouraged reporters covering venture capital news to speak with the entrepreneurs the MTDC had backed to learn their stories. We also published our complete audited financial statements as part of each year's annual report.

The public-awareness dynamic changed in 1993. The successful initial public offering by Powersoft in February 1993 created a buzz about that company, but also about the role that MTDC played in helping to finance its launch ten years earlier.

Soon a number of stories began to appear in the local media about the MTDC. For example, the February 22 to March 7, 1993, edition of *Mass High Tech (MHT)* published the first of three articles; it was entitled "State's Venture Firm Breeds Winners: This Small But Innovative Government Agency Has Paid Big Dividends." This was followed in the *MHT* edition dated March 8 to 21, 1993, by a second piece, titled "MTDC Manages Patient and Brave Money: Entrepreneur and Venture Pros Give the Quasi-Public Agency High Marks." Finally, the March 22 to April 4, 1993 *MHT* edition included an article titled "Entrepreneurs Turn to MTDC for Early Stage Money: Hodgman and Crowley Make Profits and Create Jobs by Investing in the State's Startup Companies."[39]

In the March 28, 1993, edition of the *Boston Globe*, there was an article that featured the companies from the MTDC portfolio that had gone public.[40] It listed the following firms and the number of years since the MTDC's initial investment until each company's IPO: Cambridge Analytic Associates 1, Interleaf 4, Kronos 5, Microtouch 6, Pacer Systems 4, PLC 9, Powersoft 10, and Xylogics 7.

On April 4, 1993, the *New York Times Sunday Magazine* published a featured article about Mitchell Kertzman, the CEO of PowerSoft.[41] Mitchell had become a business celebrity not only because of his cofounding of this hot, new publicly traded company but also through his leadership role in the American Electronics Association.

This public visibility was very timely in helping to create support for the MTDC Commonwealth Fund legislation, which was now under consideration in the legislature. It also let entrepreneurs know that the corporation had capital to invest and was looking for new deals. The amount of cash in the corporation's treasury had grown from about $4.2 million at the end of 1992 to $7.1 million by the end of March 1993.

FY94 to FY96 Long-Range Plan

During the spring of 1993, the board began to consider the corporation's long-range plan for the next three fiscal years. The first step was to review what had been accomplished during the twelve years since the MTDC made its first investments.

Since inception, the MTDC had made cumulative investments of about $20 million in sixty-four companies. Of these the following successful exits had taken place: fourteen had IPOs, five had been acquired, and three had bought back their stock. While there had also been realized losses, the internal rate of return was about 18 percent.

Apart from the biotechnology sector, where we had made a strategic decision that the corporation was "too small to play," most Massachusetts technology sectors were represented. The portfolio included the following percentages of companies in these industries:

- Software and services 27%
- Computer equipment and peripherals 17%
- Industrial automation 16%
- Telecommunications and data communications 13%
- Biomedical (excluding biotechnology) 13%
- Material sciences 8%
- Advanced defense systems 3%
- Environmental management 3%

About forty different firms and individuals had coinvested with the MTDC in these companies. The corporation had become a trusted and valued collaborator with private-sector venture capitalists and angel investors.

By the end of FY92, there were about 4,800 people employed among the forty-five active companies in which the MTDC had invested. This represented an increase from the 1,300 who were employed at the time of initial investments. The 4,800 jobs had a total estimated annual payroll of $199 million, yielding about $57 million in federal and $11 million in Massachusetts annual payroll-related taxes.

The long-range plan was premised on the following goals:

1. To manage an active portfolio of thirty to thirty-five companies
2. To add five to seven new companies each year
3. To add new investment capital
4. To commercialize technologies developed in the region's various research centers
5. To assist and strengthen the portfolio companies that were prepared to participate in global markets
6. To focus on regions of the state that were underrepresented in terms of economic development
7. To better coordinate with other state quasi-public entities and state agencies in the delivery of economic-development services

With these goals in mind, the board approved a plan with the following targets:

Fiscal years:	FY94	FY95	FY96
New MTDC investments:	7	6	6
Follow-on investments:	7	6	6
Dollars invested:	$3M	$2.7M	$2.7M

The staffing plan called for ten people, two more than the current level. Of these, five would be full-time-equivalent investment professionals.

Status of the Portfolio

At each board meeting the staff would provide a brief update on the status of the portfolio through what we called the Flash Report. Companies were assigned to the following categories:

> **Star**—probability of a high rate of return in the next twelve to twenty-four months;
>
> **Potential Good Return**—probability of a good rate of return in the next eighteen to thirty-six months;
>
> **Steady**—performance at a reasonable level and no near-term need for more cash;
>
> **Turnaround**—recovering from poor performance and needing more portfolio management attention and likely more cash;
>
> **Yellow Flag**—needing greater portfolio management attention, possibly more cash, and there is a risk of loss;
>
> **Red Flag**—high probability of a loss in the next twelve to eighteen months; and
>
> **Exit Completed—**an initial public offering, merger/acquisition, buyback, or other exit strategy had been completed, but the MTDC holdings had not yet been liquidated.

As of the end of FY93, the Flash Report indicated the following number of companies in each category:

- Star—1
- Potential Good Return—2
- Steady—9
- Turnaround—5
- Yellow Flag—6
- Red Flag—5
- Exit Completed—7

Over the years many of the companies in the MTDC portfolio would move through most of the different categories of the Flash Report. For example,

> AT-Com was in Yellow Flag in the spring of 1993, but moved to Star by the winter of 1993, moved to Yellow Flag, then Turnaround during 1994, and ultimately resulted in a loss in 2004.
>
> Optical Micro Systems was in Potential Good Return in the spring of 1993, moved to Yellow Flag in the summer of 1993, stayed in that category in 1994, but then returned a gain in the spring of 1995.

This movement through the Flash Report categories reflected the nature of start-up and early-stage firms. Each company was subject to the vagaries of technological developments, market entries by competitors, economic conditions, investor support or fatigue, and most important, management strengths and weaknesses. I advised the new staff members that 30 percent of what was important in their job was to pick the companies in which MTDC would invest. The other 70 percent related to how the investment was managed once it was in the portfolio. Rarely did an investment work out as was envisioned in the original business plan.

As MTDC began FY94, the portfolio included several companies that would ultimately provide very successful returns. The following are illustrations.

> One company in Star, Multilink, yielded $5,130,000 over cost.
>
> The two in Potential Good Return, Fotec and Optical Micro Systems, yielded $850,000.
>
> Three from the Steady category—Fiberspar, Tytronics, and Voicetek—yielded $2,880,000
>
> Four in Yellow Flag—IVS, Exos, Icon, and Millitech—yielded $2,100,000.
>
> Six of the companies in Exit Completed—Aseco, Endogen, Microtouch, PLC Systems, Powersoft, and Vitronics—yielded $10,950,000.

Commonwealth Fund Enacted

At the July 29, 1993, board meeting, I reported that the legislature passed and the governor signed Section 105 of Chapter 110, Massachusetts General Laws of 1993, which authorized the MTDC to create the Commonwealth Fund. It had taken almost four years since the concept of this fund was originally proposed in the fall of 1989.

The board approved an initial $1 million to be transferred from the MTDC Director's Fund to the MTDC Commonwealth Fund account. These funds were the result of gains realized from investments made from the gains returned on original MTDC investments. Now the challenge was to secure private coinvestors who would agree to have MTDC manage their participation in the Commonwealth Fund.

Investment in Minority-Owned/Led Enterprises

During the summer of 1993, Milton Benjamin, the president of the Massachusetts Community Development Finance Corporation (CDFC), approached me about the possibility of the MTDC participating in the ownership of the Minority Enterprise Investment Corporation (MEIC) that the CDFC was planning to acquire from several New England banks. The MEIC was authorized under the Federal Small Business Investment Company (SBIC) law and had been established by the banks during the credit crisis as a way to help minority-owned or -led enterprises start and grow. Apparently the banks concluded that it would be more effective to have this entity managed and run by a state-owned quasi-public corporation that had experience in financing inner-city businesses.

One of our concerns was how few technology enterprises owned or led by minority entrepreneurs had come to the MTDC for help with financing. It seemed the relatively small number of minority engineers and scientists in Massachusetts were committed to working with established companies or research and educational institutions, rather than starting new companies. On the other hand, there were many minority entrepreneurs starting new firms that were not technology-based. Because of the MTDC charter, we were not able to invest in these nontechnology firms.

The idea of the MTDC becoming a partner with CDFC and a few other quasi-public corporations in the proposed minority-focused investment fund was appealing. This new fund was named by the CDFC as the Commonwealth Enterprise Fund (CEF). At the November 17, 1993, MTDC board meeting, an investment in the CEF was approved. The other coinvestors would include CDFC, the Massachusetts Industrial Finance Agency (MIFA), and the Massachusetts Government Land Bank.

Securing Massachusetts's Computer-Technology Base

Massachusetts companies were pioneers in the development of minicomputers, applications software, networked computers, and automation systems for semiconductor manufacturing. In each of these areas, it had a robust pool of talent, making it one of the major computer-technology centers in the world. However, it did not have a large base of semiconductor design and manufacturing companies.

In 1993, the Massachusetts Microelectronics Center (MMC), part of the Massachusetts Technology Park Corporation (MTPC), formed a task force to identify and help propose sites in the Commonwealth that would be attractive to the major semiconductor companies for the construction and operation of their next-generation fabrication facilities. The executive director of the MMC, Paul Rosenbaum, perceived a unique opportunity to undertake this effort. The projections were that over the subsequent four years, as many as 120 new semiconductor facilities would be built worldwide. The talent base in Massachusetts would be a major competitive asset.

I agreed to serve on this task force, which was called the Massachusetts Semiconductor Industry Task Force, or MASIT. The MTDC had invested in several semiconductor manufacturing automation systems companies, such as Aseco, IVS, Proconics, and XRL. These and our computer hardware and software portfolio companies gave us a very good perspective on how the computer-industry base might be strengthened if a major fabrication facility were built in the Commonwealth. However, at the time, we did not appreciate the significant impact of the Internet on semiconductor design and manufacturing. Within the next fifteen years, the size and cost of semiconductor devices used in embedded computers, smartphones, and tablets would be dramatically reduced. Manufacture of these devices would move to regions of the world where the costs were cheapest.

In addition to representatives of some of the quasi-public corporations, the members of the task force included several industry personnel: Dennis Buss of Analog Devices; Tony Rea of Advanced Micro Devices; Peter Younger of Eaton Corporation; Mike Guerra of Ibis Corporation; Steve Coit of Merrill, Picard, Anderson and Eyre; and Don Walsh of Boston Edison. Over the next year we invited communities to submit proposals of appropriate sites and visited several of these. Ultimately this effort was unsuccessful. However, several years later, Intel bought the Alpha Chip fabrication facility that Digital Equipment Corporation had built in Hudson. Ultimately Intel decided to close and sell that facility in 2013.

Deals of 1993

The *Boston Globe*/Price Waterhouse survey of venture capital investment for the last quarter of 1993 reported that the following Massachusetts-based deals had closed.[42]

> *Biotech and Medical Instrumentation*: Nitromed, Middlesex Science, Pharmaceutical Peptides, Periodontix, Intra-Sonix, Innovasive Devices, Fairchild Medical Systems, Boreas, ArQule Partners, Transkaryotic Therapy, Phytera, Brunswick Medical, and American Surgical Technologies
>
> *Communications*: Steinbrecher, LANArt, and Concord Communications (MTDC)

Hardware and Peripherals: Leap Technology

Environmental: Boston Advanced Technologies

Health-Care Services: Wellmark Healthcare Services, Paldos Heathcare, Child Health Systems, and Men's Health Systems

Software: Cottage Software, Articulate Systems, Cortex, Watermark Software, Health Share Technology, Dr. T's Music Software, The Dodge Group, and Symbiotics (MTDC)

Miscellaneous: Replica, Sensitech (MTDC), Vertigo Development Group, Fixtronix, Laserdata, Holographix, Lexington Power Management, and Littlepoint (MTDC)

The deals of 1993 represented the different industry sectors that were currently in favor. These were not the type of Internet-based companies that would begin to appear in the late 1990s. It wasn't until the spring of 1994 that Mosaic Communications Corporation, later called Netscape, was founded, and the summer of 1995 before it went public. Its IPO was historic since this unprofitable company's market valuation at the end of its first day of trading was $2.9 billion. This extraordinary valuation captured the attention of investors. There was a feeling that Internet-based companies were going to offer fabulous returns in the next few years.

In 1993 venture capital investors were still doing early-stage deals and were generally managing investment funds of less than $200 million. Within a few years, many of these firms grasped the opportunity to raise significantly larger funds and make investments in a new type of company: Internet firms capturing "eyeballs" with revenue and profits yet to be realized. One of these, Cadabra, was founded in the summer of 1994 and went online as Amazon in 1995.

Stepping Up the Pace

As the MTDC began 1994, it had $8.7 million in cash, more than its initial capital, and a portfolio of over thirty companies that had not yet completed their exit strategies. In addition, the Commonwealth Fund had been authorized as a vehicle through which additional investment capital might be secured.

The coinvestor climate had also improved. In March 1994, the *Boston Globe* published an article titled "Looser Times at Start-up High: Early-Stage Investing Faucet Back On after Early 1990s Shut Off."[43] Now there were private-sector firms and individual investors actively seeking new deals in which the MTDC could collaborate.

Commonwealth Fund Coinvestors

Bob Crowley and I took the lead in pitching the Commonwealth Fund coinvestment opportunity. By March 1994, we had discussions with several potential partners, such as Fleet Bank, Bank of Boston, Massachusetts Pension Reserves Investment Management Board (PRIM, the manager of the Pension Reserve Investment Trust—PRIT), Boston Edison, Massachusetts Electric, and NYNEX.

The discussion with the executive director of PRIM was especially noteworthy. We had already managed $2 million on behalf of PRIT starting in 1986, of which about $1.4 million had already been distributed back to the agency. There were still five active companies in the PRIT/MTDC portfolio. We proposed to roll over the investments in these companies into the new Commonwealth Fund as part of PRIT's contribution as a coinvestor. Based on the current market valuation of the five companies, we offered to set this proposed contribution at $500, 000, but asked that PRIT consider adding more to this account.

The basic idea of the Commonwealth Fund had been conceived in 1989 as a vehicle to encourage PRIT to become MTDC's major coinvestor. In fact, the original proposal was that 20 percent of the net gains realized from MTDC's contribution of its assets to the fund would be distributed to PRIT. This offer had been declined. At that point, we changed the proposed beneficiary of the share of net gains to the Massachusetts General Fund.

By 1994, PRIT had invested in a number of venture capital partnerships, and its pool of assets had grown substantially. It had targeted investing at least $10 million in any one fund and limiting its participation to less than 10 percent of any one fund. Since the MTDC Commonwealth Fund proposed a total of $10 million, we were offering an opportunity that was too small for PRIT's target. Furthermore, PRIT's earlier investment in the Commonwealth Capital Ventures Partnership was viewed as meeting its commitment to an economically targeted investment (ETI) program. There was no compelling economic development or investment reason that PRIM perceived to coinvest in the MTDC Commonwealth Fund. Consequently, it declined.

The episode with PRIM highlighted the difficulty we would have raising capital for the MTDC Commonwealth Fund. We were trying to raise a fund that would be too small to attract the attention of major institutional investors. However, if we raised too large a fund, we would not be able to invest the smaller amounts that the types of firms in our target market needed. This situation underscored a fundamental problem that caused venture capital firms to move away from investing in very early-stage technology companies seeking relatively small amounts of capital. It was more efficient and profitable to raise larger funds and increase the average deal size.

The regulated utility companies—Boston Edison, Mass Electric, and NYNEX—ultimately found no compelling reason to participate in the MTDC Commonwealth Fund.

We had more success with the banks. They could include a coinvestment in the MTDC Commonwealth Fund as meeting one of their requirements under the Community Reinvestment Act (CRA). Since both Fleet Bank and Bank of Boston wanted their CRA commitments to be viewed positively by their regulators, they were willing to participate. In addition, the high-tech lending officers of these two banks were internal advocates because they understood that the types of companies MTDC backed could become future customers. Both Fleet and Bank of Boston would ultimately agree to coinvest $1 million each with $3 million from the MTDC in the Commonwealth Fund investment program.

Potential Commonwealth Fund Deals

While it would be the early summer of 1995 before the two banks executed the MTDC Commonwealth Fund legal agreements and made their funds available, the staff began to focus on potential investments. During the spring of 1994, three companies were listed on the Flash Report as "Stars": AT-Comm, Multilink, and Reflection Technology.

These three firms became initial targets since they were approaching positive exit strategies and would need to raise additional capital in the interim. This was often the time when investors could purchase shares and then sell them in the next couple of years at a large multiple of the purchase price. For example, if the shares were sold at only double the purchase price in two years, the annualized rate of return would be over 40 percent. Since the MTDC was very familiar with these companies and was already an investor, the corporation would be able to participate in the next round of financing.

The MTDC Traditional Fund had made its initial investment in AT-Comm in November 1991. This company developed one of the first automated highway toll-collection systems. By 1994, it had sold and installed systems in Illinois and other states and was working with an investment bank on a plan to go public later that year.

Multilink received its initial traditional-fund investment in September 1987. By 1994, the company had generated sales of over $17 million of its teleconferencing system. Several companies had expressed an interest in acquiring the firm, and Multilink's management thought this might take place within the next year.

MTDC's initial traditional-fund investment was made in Reflection Technology in August 1990. By 1994, the company had begun to sell its innovative miniature computer display technology to companies that were applying it in cellular phones and video-gaming systems. The company was contemplating a public offering within the next year.

However, by the time that the Commonwealth Fund investment program was launched in 1995, circumstances had changed with each of these companies. Other firms then emerged as candidates. This was typical of the rapidly shifting conditions in the early-stage technology sector.

For example, AT-Comm was advised by its investment bank to put off its public offering until 1995, when market conditions might improve. By the fall of 1994, the staff reclassified the company from Star to Yellow Flag on the Flash Report because it was running low on cash. In 1995, the company closed on a private round of investment totaling over $13 million. However, during the summer of that year, AT-Comm embarked on an ad campaign criticizing the management of the Massachusetts Turnpike Authority for planning to pick a toll-booth automation vendor with a different system design than AT-Comm's. This campaign backfired in the marketplace. While the company continued to operate for several more years, it lost its momentum. By the time it exited the MTDC portfolio in 2004, there was a loss on this investment.

FY95 to FY97 Operating Plan

At the July 21, 1994, meeting, the board approved the three-year operating plan that targeted the following number of investments:

	FY95	FY96	FY97	$ for 3 years
New Traditional Fund:	7	8	9	$6.3 million
Portfolio Follow-On:	9	13	13	$3.5 million
Commonwealth Fund:	6	6	3	$4.5 million

At the time this plan was formulated, we had no idea the Internet would have such a dramatic impact on the amount of venture capital investing that would take place in the late 1990s.

More Commonwealth Financing Programs

During the spring of 1995, the number of financing programs that included the name Commonwealth proliferated. Although the MTDC Commonwealth Fund was the first with the legislation we filed in 1990, there were now the Commonwealth Enterprise Fund and Commonwealth Capital Partners.

The Commonwealth Enterprise Fund (CEF) was the minority business-focused program in which the MTDC agreed to be a shareholder. On March 2, 1995, the MTDC closed its $600,000 investment in the CEF for 26 percent of its equity. The other partners included CDFC, 33 percent; MIFA, 26 percent; and the Land Bank, 15 percent.

Commonwealth Capital Partners was a new venture capital firm that was established with an initial combined investment of $50 million from the Massachusetts Pension Reserve Investment Trust (PRIT) and the Massachusetts State Employees and Teachers Retirement Investment Fund. It was designed to manage the economically targeted investment (ETI) program for these two funds by investing in Massachusetts companies.

One of the three founding partners of Commonwealth Capital was Steve McCormack. He had begun his career as a venture capital professional, working as an investment analyst with the MTDC in the early 1980s. The senior partner, Mike Fitzgerald, had been a general partner with Palmer Partners, a venture capital firm founded by John Shane and Bill Congleton, who had worked together at the American Research and Development Corporation (ARD), one of the first venture capital firms in the country. The third partner was Jeff Hurst, who had previously worked in private equity investing, including GE Capital's corporate finance group.

Since its founding in 1995, Commonwealth Capital Partners has gone on to raise money from limited partners beyond the two Massachusetts state pension funds. By 2013, it had $580 million under management and investments throughout the Northeast and the United States. It had evolved from a relatively small fund with a Massachusetts ETI mission to a large, financially successful investment fund that was not geographically limited.

Another initiative that was launched during the winter of 1995 was the Task Force on Emerging Companies. In the March 10–16, 1995, edition of the *Boston Business Journal*, there was an article titled "Dream Team Examines State's VC Needs."[44]The report was that the first meeting of this group was held and that among its members were: Paul Severino, MTDC board member; Steve Walske, CEO of Parametric Technology

Company (PTC); Cathy Minehan, president of the Boston Federal Reserve Bank; and Mitt Romney, managing director of Bain Capital.

Deals of 1995

The *Boston Globe*/Price Waterhouse Venture Capital Survey of investments closed in the third and fourth quarters of 1995 reported the following Massachusetts deals.[45] The companies in which MTDC invested during these two quarters are noted below.

Biotechnology/Pharmaceuticals: Archturus Pharmaceuticals, Ascent Pharmaceuticals, DigiTrace Care Services, Implemed, Innovasive Devices, Intelligene, Microsurge, Mitotix, NitroMed, Ontogeny, Sequenom, and Transcend Therapeutics

Business Services: Connected and Protocol Work Systems

Communications: American Internet, Concert Communications, Data Marine International, In Stream, SmartTel Communications, and Windata

Consumer: American Hard Cider, Belmont Gourmet International, Protocol Work Systems, and the Cornerstone Group

Distribution/Retailing: Cybersmith and Performance Polymers

Electronics and Instrumentation: Computer Numerical Controls, Design Circuits, IVS (MTDC), Seachange Technology, and Sensitech (MTDC)

Environmental: SelecTech (MTDC) and Venturi Association of Massachusetts

Hardware and Peripherals: Agile Networks, Databook, Digital Vision, VIBRINT (MTDC), VST Power Systems (MTDC), and Xionics Document Technologies

Health Care: Healthcare First, Health Share Technology, and Professional Dental Associates

Industrial: Boreas, Cambridge Applied Systems (MTDC), Gel Sciences, Powercell, and Tech Pak

Medical Instruments and Devices: Aspect Medical Systems, BioPhotonics, Focal, Innovasive Devices, MDI Instruments, Physiometrix, and Transfusion Technologies

Software and Information: Advertising Communications International, Agents, Amulet, Applied Language Technology, Avicena, Business Matters, Concord Communications, Corex Technologies, DBNEWCO, Essense Systems, Exa, Geotel Communications, Harvard Radio, High Ground Computer Storage, Market Place Information Holdings, Mesa Group, Mission Critical Technologies (MTDC), Net2Net, NetSuite, New Code Technology, Novasoft, Optimax Systems, Pendulum Design (MTDC), PSI Holding Group, REALink Systems, Solidworks, Vectis, Venturcom (MTDC), Vermeer Technologies, Vertigo Development, and Workgroup Technologies

Of all these companies, only the following indicated they were developing products related to the Internet:

American Internet (communications software)

Agents (Internet-based applications using intelligent agents technology)

Agile Networks (manufacturer of Ethernet networking and advanced switching products and telecommunications productivity software)

Amulet (Internet-based automated information retrieval service)

Avicena (health-care information services via the Internet)

Concert Communications (high-performance wide-area networking products for the information superhighway)

Connected (online services for Internet and private networks)

Cybersmith (online service and retail centers)

In Stream Corporation (electronic communications network for behavioral health sector)

Vermeer Technologies (visual client-server tools for World Wide Web)

None of the investments that MTDC made in 1995 touched on the Internet. Our portfolio continued to represent the wide array of technology enterprises in Massachusetts.

Another indicator of the pre-Internet investment environment was the type of Massachusetts-based companies that had initial public offerings (IPO) during the third quarter of 1995. The *Boston Globe* listed the following:[46]

> General Scanning, Inc. ($34.8 M raised)—laser systems for semiconductor, electronics, aircraft, and medical industries
>
> HPR Inc. ($31.4 M raised)—software and proprietary database products for the health-care industry
>
> Desktop Data, Inc. ($30 M raised)—customized real-time news and information delivered over local area networks
>
> Thermospectra Corporation ($21 M raised)—precision imaging, inspection, and measurement instruments
>
> ON Technology Corporation ($42 M raised)—groupware applications and workgroup utilities software for heterogeneous networks
>
> Hospitality Properties Trust ($187.5 M raised—acquires, owns, and leases hotel properties throughout the United States

The amounts raised by most of these firms were dwarfed by the size of the IPOs during the Internet bubble.

Capital Gap for Seed and Early-Stage Funds

By the end of 1995, seed and early-stage venture capital firms were facing challenges raising new funds. In the Winter 1996 newsletter of the law firm Testa, Hurwitz and Thibault, Richard Testa wrote an article titled "The Funding Gap for Smaller Funds." He stated:

> Small is not beautiful in the eyes of the largest institutional investors with increasing amount of capital to put to work. As a result, funds that are less than $50 million are struggling to raise capital. The bottom line is that fewer startup companies will be funded because companies with small funding requirements will have less access to venture capital.[47]

Mr. Testa's comments resonated since he was viewed as one of the most experienced legal advisors in Boston to many of the leading venture capital firms.

Pension and endowment funds assets had grown rapidly as their stock holdings increased in value. Even if they allocated only 5 percent for venture capital partnerships, the amount of dollars earmarked for their venture capital asset class might have doubled. In addition, the potential returns envisioned from venture capital investments made this class more attractive to pension and endowment fund managers. The floodgates were about to open.

From the perspective of a venture capital general partnership, having more large institutional investors in their limited partnerships was very enticing. A 2 percent management fee for a $400 to $500 million fund would yield four or five times the revenue of an earlier $100 million fund. Of course, the number of companies that could be reasonably managed would not be increased by the same multiple. The only way to put these very large funds to work would be to invest larger amounts in each company. Instead of looking for deals needing $1 million, the venture capital firms would need to find opportunities to invest $5 to $8 million in the first round.

The MTDC's plan to raise a $10 million Commonwealth Fund was flying in the face of this development. In fact, we met with Dick Testa, and he advised us to try to raise a minimum of $25 million. The problem was that if we raised a large fund, we would not be able to address the smaller capital needs of the types of companies we were chartered to back. While the deadline for raising the $10 million was delayed until June 30, 1996, we needed to close the fund-raising effort and begin investing the $5 million that had already been committed.

Private-sector venture capital firms began to raise larger funds in 1995. The Winter 1996 edition of the *Venture Capital Journal* reported that in 1995 a record $4.4 billion was raised nationally.[48] This outcome contrasted with the following amounts raised in the previous five years: $3.8 billion in 1994, $2.5 billion in 1993, $2.5 billion in 1992, $1.3 billion in 1991, and $1.8 billion in 1990. Even these amounts would seem paltry compared to the funds raised between 1998 and 2000.

In the spring of 1996, Richard Testa and Jane Morris of the Lakeside Group organized a Seed and Early Stage Alliance Trust with the goal of raising $450 to $500 million from institutional investors that would be managed by fifteen preselected seed and early-stage venture funds. MTDC was asked to apply, but ultimately, despite our strong track record, it was determined that we did not have a legal structure (e.g., limited partnership) that would fit the criteria of the trust.

By the spring of 1997, the Seed and Early Stage Alliance Trust was shelved. According to a report in the April 1997 *Private Equity Analyst*, while twenty firms had been selected, "opposition to the idea from specialized investment consulting firms was a principal obstacle."[49] The gatekeepers objected. The only state public pension fund that had made a commitment to the Seed and Early Stage Alliance Trust was Wisconsin, which had not retained a gatekeeper consultant.

CHAPTER 7

WALTZING WITH THE ELEPHANTS

From its earliest days, the MTDC had to develop a strong working relationship with the private-sector venture capital and angel investor communities. It was much easier to find coinvestment opportunities when the private-sector investors had an appetite for deals that might range from $1 to $2 million. Now many of our historic coinvestors would no longer be able to make smaller investments.

Venture Capital Players in 1996

The March 1996 edition of the *Boston Business Journal* listed the largest venture capital firms in Boston based on the amount of capital under management.[50] Below are the firms, the total dollars under management, and the number of Massachusetts-based investment professionals.

Hancock Venture Partners ($1.979 billion and twenty professionals)

Advent International ($1.7 billion and twenty-six professionals)

Summit Partners ($1.4 billion and twenty-eight professionals)

Bain Capital ($1.2 billion and forty-three professionals)

TA Associates ($1.0 billion and twenty-one professionals)

BancBoston Capital ($700 million and twenty-four professionals)

Berkshire Partners ($700 million and sixteen professionals)

Burr, Egan and Deleage ($700 million and seven professionals)

Media/Communications Partners ($450 million and eight professionals)

Greylock ($350 million and seven professionals)

Matrix Partners ($350 million and four professionals)

Weston Presidio Capital ($300 million and four professionals)

Highland Capital Partners ($280 million and six professionals)

Charles River Ventures ($265 million and six professionals)

Atlas Ventures ($250 million and seven professionals)

Bessemer Venture Partners ($250 million and seven professionals)

Capital Resource Partners ($227 million and seven professionals)

Battery Ventures ($160 million and six professionals)

Boston Capital Ventures ($151 million and six professionals)

Ampersand Ventures ($150 million and fifteen professionals)

Fidelity Ventures ($150 million and four professionals)

Marlborough Capital Advisors ($150 million and three professionals)

One Liberty Ventures ($150 million and six professionals)

GCC Investments ($140 million and three professionals)

Advanced Technology Ventures ($130 million and three professionals)

While several of these firms had been coinvestors with the MTDC in the 1980s and early 1990s, the size of their funds had grown to the point that they could no longer make small seed or early-stage investments. On the other hand, there were a number of smaller venture capital funds in the area with whom we coinvested, such as Zero Stage Capital, MDT Advisors, BU Community Technology Fund, Pioneer Capital, Kestrel Venture Management, and Claflin Capital Management. Together with angel investors and a few corporate strategic venture groups, the

MTDC was able to continue to help finance technology start-ups. However, the capital gap faced by these new firms was beginning to grow. Now companies needing to raise less than $1.5 to 2 million were having difficulty.

We were also faced with challenges arising from the limits set in our charter. For example, how would we deal with situations where our economic-development purpose might conflict with our role as financial fiduciaries? This conflict arose in the mid-1990s around one of our portfolio companies.

Littlepoint Precedent

In February 1996, the board and staff encountered the first instance when we would not be authorized to protect an earlier investment in a portfolio company. An initial investment in Littlepoint Corporation had been made in March 1993 from the MTDC Traditional Fund. The company had developed an insect repellent that was especially designed for children. It did not contain DEET, a common ingredient in other insect repellents viewed as having toxic properties. In late 1995, Littlepoint had reached an agreement to be acquired by Minnetonka Brands of Minnesota. However, in order to maintain an equity position in the new company, all the current investors in Littlepoint were required to make an investment in the new entity.

Since the new company would no longer employ staff in Massachusetts, the MTDC was not permitted to participate in this round. The MTDC enabling act required that the board find that an enterprise in which the corporation made an investment would increase or maintain employment in the Commonwealth. As a result of this limitation, the MTDC had to incur a loss.

The Littlepoint precedent applied only to Traditional Fund investments. The Commonwealth Fund enabling act did not require the same type of finding regarding employment in the state. Therefore, it would be possible to make a follow-on investment from this fund to protect an earlier investment, regardless of where the jobs were located. This had also been the case with the PRIT Fund investments. In both of these cases, the MTDC would be able to act in just the same way as any private-sector venture capital firm.

Before the Littlepoint case, only one of our portfolio companies, Vitronics, had moved out of state in the 1980s. However, by the time it relocated, it had become a publicly traded company, so we did not have to add new funds to this investment, but only liquidate our holdings over time. The need to make follow-on investments to protect our position in portfolio firms had grown during the 1990s and would continue for the foreseeable future. The Littlepoint precedent would have to be addressed by amending the MTDC charter.

Updating the Charter

While the Commonwealth Fund amendment to the MTDC enabling act in 1993 helped to address some of the limitations, the original charter would need to be revised. A major reason driving a charter update was that the Commonwealth of Massachusetts was not likely to be the source of new investment capital for the MTDC in the foreseeable future.

The last appropriation for the traditional investment fund had been in 1987. Since then, realized gains on our investments had exceeded the total of $5.2 million that the Commonwealth had originally put into the MTDC between 1980 and 1987. In addition, several of the portfolio companies were approaching their exit strategies in the next few years and would offer additional potential gains.

Given all the other demands for appropriations, it was not timely to ask the governor and legislature to add more public funds. On the contrary, there was always a risk that the legislature would seek to raid the MTDC treasury as it attempted to do in the past. Consequently, there was a strong desire among the board members and staff to diversify our sources of investment funds. To secure capital from private sources, the MTDC would need to look more like a typical venture capital firm.

It was not politically feasible to simply convert the MTDC into a private venture capital company. In addition, the tax advantages of being a public instrumentality were compelling. The MTDC could redeploy its realized gains and interest income to run its operations and replenish its investment fund without being concerned with capital gains or income taxes. It would take a creative approach to balance MTDC's historic economic-development mission with its responsibility to realize returns that would attract private investors.

Another reason for updating the charter was to find a way to create a performance-based compensation plan that would help retain key investment staff members. By the mid-1990s, we had hired and trained several new investment associates. Some of them would later leave to join private investment firms at substantially higher salaries with more robust bonus plans than the MTDC was authorized to pay. Our ability to secure private-sector investment capital was directly linked to the retention of key investment staff members.

Our experience with the legislation to create the Commonwealth Fund was that it took four years from its conceptualization in 1989 until the amendments were passed. It would take a similar length of time before the charter updates were enacted.

Follow the Money

During the last quarter of 1995 and the first quarter of 1996, the Price Waterhouse Survey of Venture Capital Investments reported in the *Boston Globe* the following numbers of venture capital firm seed or first-stage investments made in Massachusetts-based companies by industry sector:[51]

- Biotechnology and Pharmaceuticals: 4
- Business Services: 2
- Consumer: 2
- Electronics and Instrumentation: 1
- Computer Hardware and Peripherals: 1 (MTDC investment)
- Industrials: 1
- Medical Instruments and Devices: 2
- Health Care: 3
- Software: 14 (Of these, eight were Internet-related.)

Early signs of interest in Internet-related investments were beginning to appear. However, at the MTDC, we approached this new sector cautiously since it seemed that many more dollars than we had available would be needed to launch and support these types of enterprises.

Mid-1996 MTDC Portfolio

In July 1996, the MTDC portfolio included the following numbers of companies categorized by our Flash Report:

- Stars: 1 (1 eventually resulted in a gain)
- Potential Good Return: 3 (2 eventually resulted in gains)
- Steady: 11 (5 eventually resulted in gains)
- Turnaround: 4
- Yellow Flag: 5 (1 eventually resulted in a gain)

- Red Flag: 7 (1 eventually resulted in a gain)
- Exit Completed: 5 (2 eventually resulted in gains)

Of these thirty-six companies, twelve, or 33 percent, ultimately yielded gains totaling over $20 million, more than covering losses. Of the companies with positive returns, none was Internet-related. In addition, all of these thirty-six firms provided direct jobs during their multiyear tenure regardless of whether they produced gains or losses. They also purchased goods and services from local vendors that supported indirect jobs.

1996 VC and IPO activity

An article in the August 9 to 15, 1996, edition of the *Boston Business Journal* was titled "Second Quarter Shatters Record for VC Funding."[52] It reported that $425.9 million was invested in ninety-six New England companies, for an average investment per company of $4.4 million. Nationwide $3 billion was invested in 584 companies, for an average of $5.1 million per enterprise.

The top five companies in Massachusetts, each receiving $20 million of investment during the second quarter of 1996, were: Focal (medical devices), U.S. Healthworks (health care), Frontier Group (health care), Pacer Electronics (industrial distribution), and Pharmaceutical Peptides (biotechnology/pharmaceuticals). Of the other seventy-two Massachusetts companies on the *Boston Business Journal* list, only five were Internet-related.

During the third quarter of 1996, the *Boston Business Journal* reported that sixty-nine Massachusetts companies received a total of $178 million, for an average of $2.6 million per enterprise.[53] The top five were Domain Solutions—$31 million (software), Polar Corp.—$20 million (consumer), Inframetrics—$10 million (medical devices),

Maker Communications—$8.7 million (computer equipment and peripherals), and Tessara—$8 million (semiconductor). Of the other twenty-eight on the *Boston Business Journal* list that raised at least $1 million, only two were Internet-related.

In the fourth quarter of 1996 the number of seed and first-stage investment in communications companies, especially those building the Internet infrastructure, began to grow. According to the *Boston Globe*/Price Waterhouse Survey of Venture Capital Investments, there were nine companies in the communications sector that received seed and first-stage investments.[54] Of these, six were Internet-related.

The venture capital herd was beginning to smell the opportunities for big financial rewards from Internet companies. However, the focus was still largely on business-to-business enterprises. Using the Internet to fuel business-to-consumer ventures was yet to come.

The fourth quarter 1996 was also marked by a number of Massachusetts-based companies going public. According to a report in the *Boston Globe*, these included the following:[55]

- ARQuile, life sciences, raised $30 million
- Bitstream, software, raised $12.6 million
- Boston Biomedica, life sciences, raised $13.6 million
- Cubist Pharmaceuticals, life sciences, raised $15 million
- Forrester Research, business services, raised $32 million
- Geo Tel, communications, raised $26.4 million
- QC Optics, semiconductor, raised $5.8 million
- Seachange, software, raised $30 million
- Specialty Catalog, business services, raised $9.8 million
- Suburban Ostomy Supply, health care, raised $46.8 million
- Transkaryotic Therapies, life sciences, raised $37.5 million
- Visage Technology, software/hardware, raised $26.3 million
- Vivid Technologies, software/hardware, raised $24 million

- Websecure, Internet, raised $8.2 million

The fact that only one of these IPOs was for a company that was Internet-related underscores the diversity of technology firms during this period. It would still be a few years before the Internet deals began to take center stage.

Tiptoe onto the Internet

At the April 3, 1997, MTDC board meeting, a new investment in Courion Corporation was approved. Its initial product was a system to automate resetting computer passwords. While this system would be used on companies' wide area networks, it would also become applicable as more traffic moved to the Internet. The following report of Rob Frohman's interview with Chris Zannetos provides the background of this company.

> **Chris Zannetos—Courion**
>
> Founded in 1996 by Chris Zannetos and a former direct report, Courion develops identify and access management solutions which help organizations manage access risk to vital information. Mr. Zannetos showed a drive for entrepreneurship and demonstrating an unwavering interest in the business of engineering. According to Mr. Zannetos, entrepreneurship is "in the blood."
>
> Mr. Zannetos received B.Sc. degrees in Economics and Political Science from M.I.T. and a M. Sc. in Management from the M.I.T Sloan School of Business, where his thesis focused on the tie between marketing

and software product development. Wanting to continue learning about software, Mr. Zannetos joined Data General after leaving M.I.T where he drove sophisticated products to success. Typical of technology entrepreneurs, he was quickly promoted, eventually leaving Data General as a Manager of Engineering after 3.5 years.

Mr. Zannetos' decision to leave was prompted by a desire to learn the skills required to own his own company. This led Mr. Zannetos to help start Onsett International, an IT consulting firm, with a former manager from Data General. Working as program manager on a principal project, Mr. Zannetos observed that a significant portion of support calls from a client came in as forgotten passwords and requests for modified access. Having been at Onsett for over 5 years and with a desire to move back to product development, Mr. Zannetos decided to leave Onsett to found Courion with an idea.

Leaving on May 31, 1996, Mr. Zannetos left Onsett and quickly wrote a business plan around a password-reset product (and user provisioning as a second phase), eventually leading to Courion. Joining with the principal engineer of his projects from his Data General days, Courion was incorporated three weeks later, on June 19, 1996.

Initially, funding came from Mr. Zannetos and his co-founder. By October of 1996, the need for capital was apparent. Venture Capital was approached, but only no's were received. At an SBANE meeting, Mr. Zannetos met Bob Crowley and was introduced to MTDC.

Not having heard of MTDC, as the organization is not significantly self-promoting, Mr. Zannetos was interested in pursuing the funding. Eventually Courion received an Angel round of $250k and MTDC matched at $250k. In August 1997, Courion landed its first customer, though Mr. Zannetos still did not take a salary despite a family at home. Then in July 1998, Courion signed Dell Computer, which provided much needed capital. Much of it was centered on engineering, with the leadership continuing to defer salary.

In recalling the MTDC Bluebook process, he saw it as something quite powerful, in that it helped to build a "real" business plan that could be leveraged with other Venture Capital to secure funding. Seeing MTDC as closer to VC rather than Angel funding, he felt that MTDC showed entrepreneurs how to grow a business. In addition, he sees the mission of MTDC as even more relevant now than when he received initial funding. MTDC's commitment to the entrepreneur, being actively engaged in their success, had significant effect on the outcome.

Mr. Zannetos also sees that VC has gotten too big and that there is not enough seed money to bridge the gap. Here as well MTDC has a role to play, funding at the gap level. He also recounts the quasi-public nature of MTDC to be tremendously efficient. Quickly estimating the totals, Mr. Zannetos figures Courion has generated over 1000 person years of salary for Massachusetts based staff across 180 employees, totaling over $100 million in salary. He qualifies it, "Show me another government program that does that."

Courion is still in the MTDC portfolio after an initial MTDC investment was made in July 1997.[56]

At the July 17, 1997, MTDC board meeting, investments were approved in Universal Learning Technologies (later WebCT) and Andover Advanced Technologies (later Andover.net). Both of these companies would leverage the Internet in their business strategies. The following report by Rob Frohman of his interview with Carol Vallone tells the WebCT story.

Carol Vallone—WebCT

Carol Vallone was a leader and innovator from the start, growing up in an environment with fearless and supportive parents. Initially interested in becoming a teacher, she pursued a career in business receiving a B.Sc. in Business Administration.

Initially working on Wall Street and working in new product development, she observed the people around her working hard to get ahead. Looking for more, Ms. Vallone worked in marketing and analysis across several companies learning the ins and outs of sales and business. She also learned she was good at picking the winners.

Ms. Vallone eventually joined Information Mapping, where she bought into the company and served as its President. She acknowledged the business plan needed significant work, however she remarked, "Why not bet on yourself?" While at Information Mapping, Ms. Vallone learned to build vertical markets and how to reposition products. She warned, "Always be prepared for success." Wanting to grow the company, she looked for capital, as equity or in loans. In her pursuit, Ms. Vallone found a buyer for the company, however they only wanted to bring her on. She decided to leave to pursue new ventures, focusing on web-based education, launching Universal Learning Technology in 1995.

This new opportunity provided Ms. Vallone a chance to reconnect with her early desires to teach and couple it with her substantial business and product development experience. She focused on building out software tools to improve learning and help do so by connecting students and faculty. She enjoyed building out the business, especially the opportunity to define the culture.

MTDC entered in level A funding as ULT transformed into a new company named WebCT. MTDC provided the capital for a new proof of concept and to grow the business. Eventually WebCT expanded internationally in 70 countries. As the company continued to grow, they received an offer to sell, however MTDC and some of the shareholders were resistant. WebCT had confirmed the product, however there was not much confidence in the market, which crashed shortly after. Ms. Vallone admitted that while you never know what will happen, it is very hard to let go of what you have created. In 2006, WebCT was sold to competitor Blackboard.

An initial MTDC investment was made in October 1997 and MTDC exited through the sale of the company after 2006 for a net gain, per MTDC reports.[57]

Andover.net became the MTDC's most financially successful investment during the late 1990s. However, at the time when we first met Bruce

Twickler, the company's CEO, and his team, we had no idea that this would be the case.

Andover had been a software publisher. However, when the retail-software distribution system began to collapse as the Internet took over this role, the company had to reinvent itself. When they approached the MTDC, their new business model was to acquire the top websites frequented by open source, Linux, programmers. Based on the volume of traffic they had on their earliest websites, they were able to attract advertising revenue. This was at a time when advertisers were just beginning to view the Internet as a useful tool to get to target markets.

When we made the investment, we knew this was a pure Internet play. I thought this company would be sold to one of the computer industry-focused publishers in two or three years, for perhaps two or three times the initial valuation. However, the company came to us in the summer of 1999 to say they were planning an IPO in the fall, using the "Dutch auction" approach advocated by W. R. Hambrecht & Co., their lead underwriter. Furthermore, TA Associates—one of the largest private-equity firms—had committed an investment of $10 million in a mezzanine round and had asked the current investors to stand aside to let them fund the entire amount. The MTDC had invested about $600,000 in this company, along with a larger amount from private coinvestors. We decided to defer to TA since they were investing the $10 million at a much higher valuation and they would add credibility to the company when it went public.

On December 8, 1999, Andover.net went public at $18 per share. By the end of the day, the closing share price was $63.38, which valued the company at $950 million. On paper, MTDC's $600,000 investment was valued at over $43 million. However, as an inside investor, we agreed to "lock up" the sale of any stock for six months.

In March 2000, Andover.net was acquired for stock by VA Linux, a company that went public within a couple days of Andover's IPO. Unfortunately, the spring of 2000 is when the Internet bubble burst. The value of the VA Linux stock fell substantially. By the time we were free from the lockup in June 2000, we sold all of our stock in this company and realized a gain of over $12 million.

These early steps into the world of Internet-related companies taught several lessons: (1) luck is always a factor, (2) deep financial pockets make a difference, and (3) new technology rapidly changes the game. For a venture firm that had the ability to be very patient, this experience would become very important.

Claflin Deal Structure

It's noteworthy that in both the case of Andover.net, which had its IPO in 1999, and Powersoft in 1993, the investments were structured with most of the purchase in the form of nonconvertible preferred stock and a small portion of common shares. This was often the prescribed structure of Claflin Capital Management, our coinvestor in these two companies.

The rationale was that if a company did not achieve a successful exit through an IPO or merger/acquisition, the nonconvertible preferred stock would be redeemed with a cumulative dividend. This scenario would result in the return of investment capital and some income. On the other hand, if the company had a successful IPO, the common shares might yield a very high return. In these cases, the gains realized by the MTDC were the first and second largest in its history through 2001.

Cash Is King

At the beginning of 1997, there was about $3 million in cash in the MTDC treasury. The harvests of 1993 had brought the cash balance to a high of about $9 million. Over the next three years, as new investments were made, the cash balance was reduced to about $3.7 million by the end of 1996. The balance would continue to be reduced because of investments in new companies until it hit a low of about $1 million in September 1997. Fortunately, there were new harvests on the horizon. While we could never be absolutely sure these potential gains would be realized, our past experiences told us that there was a strong possibility of this happening within a few months.

In April 1997 PictureTel announced its acquisition of Multilink, an MTDC portfolio company since 1987. MTDC would receive PictureTel stock, which had the potential of yielding a $6.6 million gain. However, it would be several months before we would be able to sell this stock, and during that time its value would fluctuate.

By the fall of 1997, Concord Communication, an MTDC portfolio company since 1993, went public. In October 1997, we sold about 47 percent of our stock, yielding almost $2 million.

In October 1997, Schlumberger acquired IVS, an MTDC portfolio company since 1988, through a stock purchase. In November 1997, the value of Schlumberger's stock would have yielded the MTDC a potential gain of $2.2 million.

In the summer of 1997, these projected harvests enabled the MTDC board to authorize an investment plan for FY98 to FY00 that called for the following each year:

New Traditional MTDC Fund Investments:	6 to 8	$2,000,000
MTDC Portfolio Follow-On Investments:	10 to 15	$1,500,000

Commonwealth Fund Investments	3 to 5	$1,200,000*
Total		$4,700,000

*$720,000 from MTDC and $480,000 from coinvestors

Regional Venture Capital

In February 1997, Tom Chmura, vice president for economic development of the University of Massachusetts, wrote the following in his published report.

> The first venture capital fund ever developed in Western Massachusetts—the **Mass Ventures Equity Fund**—was established in December 1996 with $15 M of privately raised funds. It will focus on commercializing UMASS Amherst technology and includes a $1.5 million investment from the UMASS Foundation.[58]

The March 21 to 27, 1997, edition of the *Boston Business Journal* reported the first closing of $13 million for the Mass Ventures Equity Fund, which was to be managed by Mass Ventures and Kestrel Venture Management.[59] The article said the following:

> Included in the $13 million committed to the fund are investments from Massachusetts Mutual Life Insurance Co., Fleet Financial Group, the University of Massachusetts Foundation, Baystate Health Systems Inc., Springfield Institutions of Savings, American Saw and Manufacturing, the Bank of Western Massachusetts, and several other individual investors.

The seeds of this initiative were planted in the early 1990s. In 1992, I had met with the then-president of the University of Massachusetts, Michael

Hooker, and learned of his appreciation of the role of entrepreneurship and venture capital in economic development. With his encouragement, I met with the then-dean of the School of Management of UMASS Amherst, Tom O'Brien, and later with Jamie Chernoff from the UMASS Amherst chancellor's office. The purpose of these meetings was to stimulate a discussion of how to encourage the commercialization of technology developed at UMASS Amherst through entrepreneurial companies.

In 2012, the MTDC changed its name to MassVentures, but has no relationship to the Mass Ventures Equity Fund.

CHAPTER 8

EVOLVING THE MODEL

Charter Change

As the venture capital environment began to change in the late 1990s, the MTDC reexamined the business model that it followed from its inception in 1978. In 1998, it would reach its twentieth anniversary, having demonstrated great success.

It had survived a potential stillborn birth by securing investment capital from the federal government and then leveraging the federal funds to obtain investment capital from the Commonwealth. The private coinvestor community developed respect for its board and staff and joined in dozens of deals. It invested in companies that employed thousands of Massachusetts citizens. By its tenth anniversary in 1988, it had become financially self-sufficient. It had developed programs such as the PRIT and the Commonwealth Funds, through which it managed investment on behalf of others.

The board and staff began to look at whether the MTDC would continue to play a relevant role if it did not have access to predicable pools of new investment capital. Since the Commonwealth did not seem to be a likely source of these funds, the MTDC would need to find a way to attract institutional investment limited partners. These potential investment partners would be reluctant to hire the MTDC given its status as an economic-development agency of the state unless they could be assured that the MTDC's investment goals were the same as those of private venture capital partnerships, namely, to realize high rates of return. In addition, these partners would want to know that the key investment professionals would be committed to the MTDC for many years.

As indicated earlier, the MTDC had substantial tax benefits from being a public instrumentality. In addition, its personnel costs were much lower than those of private venture capital firms due to limits on compensation for public employees. These economic advantages made it feasible for the MTDC to focus on smaller investment transactions in very early-stage companies and be very patient about the timing of its harvests. The MTDC could scout out opportunities that would be appealing to larger venture capital firms once the companies had developed.

The challenge would be to find a way to modify MTDC's business model to try to bridge its mission as a public instrumentality with its expertise as a venture capital firm. The charter change legislation would be the vehicle to do this.

On May 12, 1997, I sent a letter to the then-chair of the House Committee on Science and Technology, Representative Lida Harkins, on behalf of House Bill 4429, which proposed language that would update and correct sections of Massachusetts General Law Chapter 40G that pertained to the MTDC. In this letter I described the history of the MTDC and summarized the current situation as follows:

> These stages of the MTDC's history have taken place against the backdrop of the rapid growth of venture capital in the early 1980s, the slump in venture capital after the 1987 crash, the drought of venture capital during the 1990 to 1993 credit crunch and the recent

> flood of venture capital over the past two years. Through all these periods, the capital gap faced by seed and early-stage technology companies has become chronic.
>
> The growth of assets among institutional investors such as pension funds has increased the amount of money concentrated in large venture capital firms. These firms now find it economically impractical to make small investments of under $1 million in new technology-based companies that will take 6 to 10 years to grow to the point that they yield significant financial returns.
>
> The MTDC, on the other hand, has consistently focused on these small, new companies—the mainstream of technology-oriented businesses arising from our universities, laboratories, and mature technology companies.[60]

In this letter I also commented on House Bill 4430, which would create a Massachusetts Technology Enterprise Fund that would be managed by a new organization and board of directors. I suggested that the language of the bill be amended to assign responsibility to an existing public instrumentality such as the MTDC. By September 1997, the language of this proposed legislation was amended to designate the MTDC as the responsible agency and called for $15 million to be appropriated during fiscal year 1998. Unfortunately, this proposed Technology Enterprise Fund bill was not enacted.

By 1997 it had been a decade-long effort to find a source of predictable investment capital for the MTDC. Over these years, the Commonwealth seemed ambivalent about whether to provide these funds. We would go from periods when there were inklings of support to times when the MTDC treasury would be a target for distributions. Only the success of the investment program in generating substantial returns would keep the corporation viable. We would need to find private-sector sources of capital that would be attracted by our past financial success and unique position in the Massachusetts start-up and early-stage company deal flow.

Trends in Venture Capital Investing

The *Boston Globe* Venture/PWC Money Tree reported that for the last two quarters of 1997 and all four quarters of 1998, there were relatively modest numbers of seed or first-stage investments in Massachusetts companies.[61] In 1997, there were nine in Q3 and twenty-one in Q4. In 1998 there were twenty-three in Q1, twenty-seven in Q2, twenty-nine in Q3, and twenty in Q4.

Of those new deals in Q3 of 1997, 44 percent were software companies, and only 11 percent were communications, telecom, or networking companies. There was only one Internet-related company that quarter.

By Q4 of 1997, software investments comprised 21 percent; communications, telecom, or networking companies were 19 percent; and there was only one Internet-related firm.

In Q1 of 1998, 48 percent of the deals were in software; 13 percent in communications, telecom, or networking; and only one Internet deal.

In Q2 of 1998, software companies comprised 41 percent of the deals; communications, telecom, or networking companies were 26 percent; and there were two Internet-related companies.

During Q3 of 1998, 38 percent of the investments were in software companies, and 31 percent were in communications, telecom, or networking companies. There were four Internet-related deals.

Finally, in Q 4 of 1998, software companies comprised 40 percent of the deals, and 30 percent were in communications, telecom, or networking firms. There were only two Internet-related deals.

The wildly successful initial public offering by Netscape in August 1995 is often cited as the opening bell for the Internet-related company investment race. However, it would take a few years for this sector to become red-hot. The Netscape case was used as an illustration by many venture capital firms to help them raise new funds to invest in these types of companies. The upcoming feeding frenzy on Internet-related companies would underscore the tendency of venture capitalists to act like a herd. This behavior was seen before. For example, in the 1980s, venture capital firms were financing multiple competitive computer hardware and peripheral companies.

At the MTDC we had to stay focused on our geographic niche and continue to back companies that were overlooked by the herd. Together with the relatively small size of our investment pool, we were not going to plunge deeply into the Internet-related company sector. However, we were to soon learn that many of our portfolio companies began to leverage the web, and we would need to pay close attention to the business-model implications of the Internet.

Incentives for Staff Retention

The issue of staff retention was becoming a concern as we saw the venture capital funds grow and add personnel. We had already lost Mike O'Malley to another venture capital firm. Bob Creeden, Will Wilcoxson, and others we trained were prime candidates to be recruited by private venture capital firms at much higher compensation levels. These investment staff members performed exactly the same functions as younger venture capital partners would. Furthermore, their talents and skills were well-known because of their collaboration with private coinvestors in each of our portfolio companies.

In the past, we felt that the loss of investment staff members to private venture capital firms was offset to some degree by the potential of these firms becoming coinvestors in our deals. However, as the VC funds began to grow, it was less likely that they would continue to be interested in small start-up company MTDC deals. Now we needed to retain key staff for the long term in order to attract institutional investors for the Commonwealth Fund.

In late 1997 the MTDC board directed its finance committee and me to develop a gain-sharing plan that would provide incentive compensation to encourage retention of key staff members. The model we looked at was the "carried interest" component that applied to VC general partners. In addition to an annual management fee of about 2 percent of committed capital, VC general partners would receive about 20 percent of the net gains from the investments of a fund they managed.

By spring 1998, a gain-sharing award plan was developed and approved by the board, contingent on the filing of legislation that would update the MTDC charter. The goal was to shift the status of the MTDC from being a public instrumentality to a public-purpose corporation that could operate in many of the same ways as a private VC firm. The plan called for up to 10 percent of the net gains of the corporation in a given year to be allocated to a gain-share award pool that would be earned by staff members based on their responsibilities and performance. The plan also included substantial forfeiture penalties if a staff member left the corporation.

Since the vehicle for managing private institutions' funds would be the MTDC Commonwealth Fund Investment Program, 20 percent of annual net realized gains from the MTDC's portion of that fund would be paid to the Commonwealth's general fund. For example, in July

1998, the MTDC distributed $201,166 to the general fund based on net realized gains in FY98. If the MTDC could retain key staff, attract private institutional dollars, and achieve strong financial returns, then the Commonwealth would not only benefit from new job creation, but also receive a direct financial return.

Celebrating the Twentieth Anniversary

On November 10, 1998, the MTDC hosted a reception for its portfolio company entrepreneurs, its coinvestors, public officials, and members of the high-technology community to celebrate the twentieth anniversary of its founding. The key accomplishments that were cited included the following:

1. Thirty-five million dollars had been invested in ninety Massachusetts companies. This amount was a multiple of 4.3 times original capital. The income, gains, principal payments, and capital returns on the $8.2 million of original investment funds paid for all operating expenses and recycled surpluses into new investments.
2. Eight thousand six hundred people were employed among the active current and former portfolio companies. This aggregation of jobs would rank the combined MTDC companies among the top fifty private employers in the Commonwealth.
3. Four hundred thirty-one million dollars in total annual payroll was being paid.
4. Nineteen million dollars in annual payroll-related tax revenue went to the Commonwealth
5. One hundred thirty-one million dollars in annual payroll-related tax revenue went to the federal government.
6. Four hundred thirty-nine million dollars of both initial and subsequent private coinvestment was made in the portfolio

companies. This represented about $12.50 of private-sector money for every $1 of public-sector funds.

7. Twenty-two million dollars of net gains were realized. Gross realized gains were $32 million, coming from fourteen companies that went public, twelve that were acquired, and five that bought back their stock.

At the time, the active MTDC portfolio represented the following industry sectors:

- Computer software and services: 9 companies
- Computer equipment and peripherals: 4 companies
- Industrial automation systems and equipment: 4 companies
- Biomedical investments: 4 companies
- Telecommunications and data communications: 3 companies
- Material science and environmental management: 4 companies
- Internet-related: 3 companies

On September 30, 1998, there was over $10 million in cash in the corporation's treasury. The board had approved an operating plan for the fiscal year ending June 30, 1999, that called for investments from the traditional MTDC fund in six new companies to the portfolio and ten follow-on cases, as well as adding two new companies and two follow-on cases from the Commonwealth Fund. We had a complement of five full-time-equivalent investment staff members. In short, we were prepared for a very active FY99, and the forecast for the next few years looked positive.

The charter-change legislation had been drafted and would be filed with the legislature by December 1, 1998.

Among the key technical changes included language that would:

1. add to the corporation's powers the ability to participate as a general partner or a limited partner in a limited partnership and to participate as a member or manager in a limited liability corporation;
2. add to the employment-creation criteria that the companies MTDC financed would employ individuals undertaking job retraining as a consequence of technological change or corporate restructuring;
3. increase the limit to be invested in any one company from $500,000 to $1 million, and authorize the board to periodically adjust the limit based on the changes in the annual inflation rate; and
4. remove current restrictions, such as the limit to 49 percent of the ownership of an individual company, the limit of not more than 20 percent of MTDC assets to be made as direct investment without coinvestors, and the requirement that at least 50 percent of MTDC investment for the previous year be made in enterprises located in certain target communities defined by statute.

With the filing of this bill, the contingency requirement in the gain-share plan was met, and awards were made to employees based on the FY98 realized net gains.

CHAPTER 9

THE INTERNET ERA ARRIVES

Inflating the Bubble

In the fourth quarter of 1997, venture capital firms across the country invested $4.5 billion in 918 deals, for an average of $4.9 million per transaction. By the first quarter of 2000, $28.4 billion was invested in 2,161 deals, for an average of $13.1 million per transaction. This quarter would be the historic peak of venture capital investing, which would see $177.6 billion invested in 15,627 deals between the second quarter of 1999 and the second quarter of 2001, for an average of $11.6 million per transaction.[62]

The race among venture capital firms to fund Internet-related companies was in high gear by the spring of 1999. The number of business-to-consumer deals proliferated. Companies like Boo.com, EToys, Pets.com, Flooz, and Webvan raised tens of millions of dollars, much of which was lost when the dot.com bubble burst.

The headline of the February 14, 1999, Venture Capital Report in the *Boston Globe* was "Two Golden Words: Internet Related."[63] The story reported that there was $561 million invested by venture capital firms in ninety-nine New England companies during the fourth quarter of 1998.

Of these, forty-one were "Internet-related" enterprises. The average deal size increased to $5.7 million.

The February 1999 edition of the *Venture Capital Journal* reported that venture capital partnerships received commitments in 1998 totaling $22.2 billion.[64] Pension funds had contributed more than half of these. The amount of dollars placed with venture capital partnerships had been rapidly accumulating. In 1999 these would flow fast and furiously into new companies leveraging web technology.

In Massachusetts, venture capital investments in Internet-related companies began to increase in the first quarter of 1999, with seven of the twenty deals made in this sector. The pace of investments in Internet companies accelerated in Q2, with fifteen of thirty-two deals; Q3, with eleven of thirty-one deals; and Q4, with fourteen of twenty-six investments. The focus on Internet-related deals increased again in Q1 of 2000, with thirty-three of forty-eight companies. In Q 2 of 2000, the number was twenty-five of forty-seven companies. However, after the Internet bubble burst in March 2000, the pace began to decrease, with twelve of twenty-nine in Q3 and ten of thirty-eight in Q4 investments being made in this sector.

MTDC Wades in

By the spring of 1999, the investment staff identified new Internet-related companies. These included SiteScape and Sprockets, both of which would join the portfolio by the end of the year.

SiteScape had developed a platform through which employees in diverse locations could more effectively communicate with one another and easily share content. Novell acquired this company in 2008, and the MTDC realized a gain.

Sprockets aspired to create a web-based platform through which customers, graphic designers, copywriters, editors, and printers could update and revise publications electronically. This approach would reduce the amount of time involved in physically moving drafts, designs, and proofs among the various parties before a final version was printed. In addition to the technical challenges faced by this company, the management made some critical mistakes very early after it received its financing. For example, it hosted a very expensive company-announcement reception for people in the publishing and printing community in Boston long before a working version of its platform was ready to go to market. By 2002, this company had ceased operations, and the MTDC realized its largest loss.

While these Internet-related companies were added to the portfolio, other new investments in 1999 included AdvantaCare, Clarity, and VisionScope, Unfortunately, only one of these three companies ultimately resulted in a gain, and for that firm it was very modest.

As mentioned earlier, in December 1999, Andover.net had a very successful IPO. The potential gain for the MTDC on paper was so great that it seemed to confirm the widespread notion that Internet-related deals would be very successful. At the same time, the MTDC systematic investment process offered a much slower pace in making investment commitments than private venture capital firms. At times, it must have seemed to some entrepreneurs that the corporation was a "dinosaur."

On paper, the value of the Andover.net stock owned by the MTDC was over $43 million on the day it went public in December 1999. However, this potential windfall did not alter our investment policies and practices. We still had to meet the requirements of our charter. We would still be limited to $500,000 as an initial investment in any new company. We could not start to invest millions of dollars per deal. In addition, we would continue to follow our tried-and-true investment process.

Winning eyeballs was the metric of success for many of the dot.com start-ups. Our metric was whether revenue would exceed expenses within a few years after our initial investment. Of course, we would make some mistakes, and some companies never achieved a positive cash flow. Many had to be sold at a loss or shut down. However, the amount we lost in a single deal would be dramatically less than that experienced by many venture capital firms during these years. On the other hand, our scores would be more like singles and doubles, not home runs.

It would not be until 2000 that the MTDC waded deeper into the Internet pool. During that year, eleven companies were added to the portfolio. Of these, three were explicitly Internet-related, while several others leveraged the web for marketing purposes. Only one of the three Internet companies contributed a gain. By the time the bubble burst in the spring of 2000, the MTDC's approach of having a diversified industry sector portfolio would be seen as a wise strategy. Furthermore, the investment process checked any temptation by the MTDC to invest as impulsively as other venture capital firms.

Beginning the New Millennium

At the June 10, 1999, MTDC board of directors meeting, the proposed operating plan for the next three fiscal years was discussed and approved. On June 30, 1999, the treasury had about $10 million in cash, more than the original $8.2 million that came into the corporation between 1980 and 1988. The market value of the portfolio was approximately $14.4 million.

Since the MTDC Commonwealth Fund I had been fully invested, we made plans to raise a new fund, MTDC Commonwealth Fund II. The second Commonwealth Fund would be similar to the first in terms of investment strategy and structure. However, we targeted raising about three times the money closed in the first. In developing the three-year investment plan, we included projections for investments made from this second Commonwealth Fund.

The investment plan for FY00 through FY02 was to make eighteen new MTDC traditional fund investments totaling $6.3 million and thirty follow-on investments in portfolio companies totaling $5.1 million. In addition, we planned to make fourteen new Commonwealth Fund II investments totaling $7 million and seven follow-on investments totaling $1 million over the same three years.

In order to expand our reach in regions of the state where the deal flow had been less robust, we retained two business-development representatives. Their mission was to increase the MTDC's visibility and scout for new investment opportunities. Mary Makela, a former MTDC board member, would cover the southeast, and Carol Brennan, an associate with the Massachusetts Business Development Corporation, would be responsible for the western region.

This bullish investment plan was formulated before we had any idea that the Internet bubble would burst a year later. In addition, we underestimated the willingness of institutional investors to commit relatively small amounts of money to the type of fund we would be trying to raise.

Some early signs of trouble ahead began to appear later in 1999. On August 18, 1999, the *Boston Globe* published an article titled "Too Venturesome? Fast Pace of Financing Deals Has Some Investors Worried." The article suggested that the role of Internet-based companies was a having a big impact. The writer, Ron Rosenberg, drew a comparison between how venture investors behaved in 1989 versus 1999. For example, the size of multistage investments before an IPO in 1989 ranged from $10 to $15 million, but in 1999 the range was $50 to $100 million. The period over which the rounds of investments were made in 1989 was two to four years, but in 1999 the range was six months to two years. Most significantly, the time to make an investment decision in 1989 was three months, but in 1999 it was three weeks.[65]

Melting Ice-Cream Cones

The rapid deterioration of value of an investment is often likened to an ice-cream cone melting in the sunlight. During the first half of 2000, many venture capital-backed investments melted down. The MTDC portfolio of publicly traded companies was not immune to this phenomenon. For example, at the end of February 2000, the potential gains on paper were $29.6 million for Andover.net; and $8.8 million for Telaxis (formerly Millitech), which had an IPO in early 2000. By June 5, 2000, VA Linux had acquired Andover.net for stock, and the potential gain for MTDC's holdings was $12.1 million. Our Telaxis stock was valued on that date at $5.7 million, but would plummet to $533,000 by October 9, 2000, then drop to a loss of $119,000 by November 6, 2000.

The lockup period for the VA Linux (Andover.net) investment ended in June 2000. We then sold all of our stock and realized a gain of about $12.7 million. Unfortunately, by the time the lockup ended for Telaxis, its value had dropped so low that a sale would have resulted in a loss. Eventually, the MTDC realized a small positive return of about $350,000 on this investment when the exit was completed in 2002.

Despite the meltdown in valuations, the number of jobs among the active current or former MTDC portfolio companies remained high. As of December 31, 1999, the estimated number based on company reports was 10,000 among fifty-five firms. By December 31, 2000, the number was 10,500 among sixty firms. The average number of jobs per company in 1999 was 182, and in 2000 it was 175. A few of the former portfolio companies had grown their employment to more than a thousand, and many to several hundred.

FY2000 Investments

For the fiscal year ended June 30, 2000, the MTDC committed $3.65 million from its Traditional Fund to ten new companies and $2.772 million for follow-on investments in portfolio companies. These numbers exceeded the plan that was established in June 1999. At that time we had not anticipated the very large gain that would be realized from the VA Linux (Andover.net) investment. The board and staff felt that it was timely to put the funds from this harvest to work in the companies that came before us during winter and spring of 2000.

In July 2000, the Flash Report categorized the following investments as Stars or Potential Good Returns, offering potential positive harvests in the next twelve to twenty-four months: VenturComm, WebCT, MicroE, and Nexcen. VenturComm would ultimately result in a small loss when the exit was completed in 2005. WebCT would be sold to Blackboard and yield two times the investment in 2006. MicroE would exit in 2004 and yield a 10.8 times return. Nexcen would result in a loss. Some of the companies that were classified as Steady would ultimately return gains, for example, Bitpipe, Sensitech, Fiberspar, and SiteScape.

It was very difficult to predict winners and losers when investing in innovative early-stage companies. The average time a company would be in the MTDC portfolio was about seven years. Many changes in technology, competition, management, finance, and economic conditions would take place over that period. However, all of these firms continued to provide employment and purchase goods and services from local vendors during these years.

After the Bubble Burst

While stock market valuations for Internet-related companies dropped swiftly in the spring of 2000, it would take several months before high expectations for these types of companies began to wane. The *Boston Globe*/PWC Money Tree Venture Capital Reports for 2000 indicated that seed and first-stage investments in Internet-related companies continued at a strong pace. For example, during the first quarter of 2000, the number of new Internet-related companies receiving venture capital dollars was thirty-three, representing 69 percent of all new Massachusetts firms backed by VCs. The number and percentages in each of the subsequent quarters of 2000 were: second quarter twenty-five, representing 53 percent; third quarter twelve, representing 41 percent; and fourth quarter ten, representing 26 percent. By the end of the year, the venture capital herd was beginning to leave the Internet pasture.[66]

What also became evident was that IPO exits by Internet-related companies were much less promising. Part of the MTDC record gain from the VA Linux (Andover.net) IPO would be recognized in FY01, because the sale of the stock took place in July. However, after that gain, the MTDC would realize poor harvests over the next few years.

The collapse of the dot.com bubble closed the window of opportunity for IPOs in the early 2000s. In addition, the Sarbanes–Oxley Act of 2002 imposed requirements on publicly traded companies that made it unfeasible for very small companies to undertake an IPO. In fact, according to the MTDC annual reports, the last time one of the portfolio companies completed an exit through an IPO was in FY03. Most of the harvests were accomplished through mergers or acquisitions. Historically this type of exit yielded far less gains than an IPO.

There were also significant losses that were realized in the early 2000s, especially in FY01 and FY02. During these years, most venture capital firms were dealing with the fallout from the collapse of the dot.com bubble. MTDC was not an exception. New companies were not meeting their revenue goals and needed more cash to survive. Venture investors were busy tending to their portfolio companies and not taking on new firms. Consequently, many companies had to be sold at a loss or shut down.

Fortunately, Massachusetts's technology entrepreneurs continued to launch new enterprises in industry sectors other than the Internet. The optimism and innovative problem-solving drive of these entrepreneurs would not be deterred by the financial setbacks facing most venture capitalists. However, once again, the capital gap facing MTDC types of companies began to widen. During these years the situation could be described as a capital drought.

The MTDC was in the same position of most venture capital firms, needing to invest more money in its current portfolio. For example, more than half of the eleven new companies that were added in FY00 would need subsequent rounds of financing. Furthermore, the investment staff would need to devote more time to taking care of their current portfolio companies. There would be less time available to bring new investments to the board.

MTDC Refocuses

In addition to tending to the portfolio companies, the MTDC added four new companies in FY01. However, none of them was Internet-related.

By the fall of 2000, one of our investment staff members had identified a company called TerraTherm. The company had acquired the rights to technology from the University of Texas. The university was the beneficiary of this intellectual property developed in the late 1990s by a division of Royal Dutch Shell. TerraTherm was now selling and installing systems that applied very high temperature to remediate toxic soil on-site.

At the time, the company was located in Fitchburg, Massachusetts, which was not viewed by venture capitalists as a high-technology community. It was providing an innovative solution to clean up hazardous waste sites in situ. While these types of cleanups represented a large market opportunity, the business model did not forecast extremely rapid growth. The founders, Ralph Baker and John Bierschenk, were skilled technologists, but not proven entrepreneurs. Finally, the amount of money they were seeking was relatively modest. In short, it met all of the MTDC's peculiar investment criteria. This investment would be approved by the board and closed in January 2001.

A dozen years later, in August 2013, TerraTherm was named in the Zweig Letter 2013 Hot Firm List as one of the fastest-growing US environmental consulting firms.[67] This was the second time the firm had been recognized by this prestigious letter. The company relocated a bit farther west of Fitchburg to the city of Gardner and now installs its systems in sites around the world. It is still run by Ralph Baker and John Bierschenk.

In February 2001, the MTDC closed an investment in CASTion, a wastewater treatment and chemistry recovery system. This company was acquired by ThermoEnergy Corporation, which continues to sell and install the original system developed by CASTion.

Two other new companies were added to the portfolio in FY01: Market Perspectives and Biofertec. Tragically, the founder of Market Perspectives, Judith Larocque, was on one of the planes that crashed into the World Trade Center on September 11, 2001. Her innovative market research firm ceased operations. Biofertec was an infertility treatment firm that became Medelle and continued in the MTDC portfolio for several years.

Transition to 2001

By the fall of 2000, the pace of venture capital investments had slowed. The December 2000 PWC Money Tree Report indicated that during the third quarter of 2000, investments in New England-based companies totaled $1.9 billion, down 29 percent from the previous quarter. The average deal size was $12.9 million, down by $2.3 million from the second quarter. Nationally the total investments in the third quarter were $17.6 billion, down 11 percent from the $19.8 billion in the previous quarter. Internet-related deals were down 29 percent from the second quarter and 41 percent from the first quarter.[68]

Silicon Valley continued to lead the regions in VC investments during the third quarter, with $6.9 billion, followed by New England with $1.9 billion, the New York Metro with $1.1 billion, and Texas with $1.1 billion. The list of the top ten most-active New England VC firms in the third quarter that was published in the PWC Money Tree Report included:

	Deals	Dollars
Bessemer Venture Partners	20	$45.8M
BancBoston Capital and Ventures	16	$40.3M
Battery Ventures	14	$76.1M
Greylock	13	$73.4M
Advanced Technology Ventures	18	$31.0M
OneLiberty Ventures	12	$12.5M
CMGI@Ventures	11	$43.9M
Matrix Partners	9	$70.7M
Charles River Ventures	9	$32.0M
VIMAC LLC	9	$ 7.0M

The MTDC was lower on this list, with four deals and $2.2 million committed.

As of December 31, 2000, the MTDC treasury had a cash balance of $14.4 million. In January 2001, Governor Cellucci appointed Drew Hannah to fill a vacancy on the MTDC board. The investment staff had a total of five full-time equivalents. The corporation was poised to continue an aggressive investment program.

Gain-Share Plan Controversy

During May and June of 2000, the state auditor sent a team to the MTDC to specifically review the gain-share award plan that had been previously adopted. The particular issue they had was whether the implementation of the plan was dependent on the filing versus the passage of legislation updating the charter of the MTDC. The board of directors had approved the implementation based on the filing of the bill, with the understanding that best efforts would be made to secure its passage.

On January 19, 2001, we received the report of the state auditor based on the fieldwork it conducted the previous year. The report contained several factual errors and incorrect interpretations; the most important of these pertained to the requirement about the filing of the legislation. Before we had the opportunity to respond to the report, which was the usual procedure in the past, the state auditor released the matter to the media.

On January 25, 2001, the auditor's office issued a press release titled "DeNucci Questions Proposed Financial Bonuses for Two Officers of Tech Corp."[69] The release recommended that the legislature, in considering the proposal to amend the MTDC's enabling law, review whether these bonuses were reasonable, warranted, and fiscally prudent. The specific gain-share awards that were cited were those made to me as president and Bob Crowley as executive vice president.

The MTDC board disagreed strongly with the auditor's report and filed a letter of response. The board had the legal authority and responsibility for determining whether the compensation plan was reasonable, warranted, and fiscally responsible. It had initiated the development of the plan, spent a significant amount of time reviewing it, discussed the plan with high-level officials in the state government, and approved its implementation. This was the first time in the MTDC history that another agency of the Commonwealth had so aggressively engaged in criticizing the action of its board of directors.

What was most puzzling about this action on the part of the auditor was that the MTDC had been extraordinarily successful in accomplishing its mission over many years. For example, by FY00 the $5.2 million of investment capital from the Commonwealth and the $3 million from the federal government had been reinvested 5.5 times, net realized gains totaled $28.5 million, and there were over 10,500 jobs among the sixty active companies that the MTDC helped to finance.

To some degree the economic climate in 2000 may have contributed to the situation. The Internet bubble had burst, and a national recession began. "However, in the collapse of the dot.com bubble in the national recession of 2001, Massachusetts was the hardest hit among the New England economies, as growth abruptly plummeted to 1.7% in 2001. Continued weakness in national business investment and in equity markets continued to impede economic growth in Massachusetts in 2002."[70] The public that had celebrated the success of the technology sector as the Internet bubble inflated became uneasy as jobs were being lost in the aftermath.

Once again the ambivalence among some public officials about the MTDC would manifest itself. There was little appetite for providing more investment capital from the Commonwealth, as well as inertia to enact the charter changes that were necessary to enable the corporation to secure private-sector funds.

It would take a few more years before the MTDC charter-change legislation would pass. The modifications were enacted by the legislature on December 23, 2002, and signed into law by Acting Governor Swift on January 1, 2003. Ultimately the board decided to discontinue the gain-share award plan in fiscal year 2006, after several years when there were no significant realized gains.

Decision to Retire

In February 2001, I decided to take an early retirement from the MTDC. While I had originally planned to retire in 2004 when I would have completed twenty years with the corporation, my wife's untimely illness and death in 2000 caused me to accelerate my decision. I wanted to explore other career options, one of which was to continue to teach entrepreneurship courses at Tufts University. I had started to teach one course each year in 1997 and enjoyed working with students very much.

I agreed to stay on until the end of the fiscal year on June 30, 2001, while the board organized a search committee to find my replacement. In April my retirement was publicly announced. The search process took longer than expected, so in July I made it clear that I wanted to leave no later than September 30.

By September, Frank Pinto agreed to become the MTDC's next president. He had several years of experience with a venture capital firm called Boston Millennia Partners and had been an entrepreneur. Unfortunately, Frank decided to resign within a relatively short period of time. The board then asked my former deputy Bob Crowley to take on the role initially ad interim, but soon after appointed him president in 2002. He served with distinction until he retired in 2011, having spent thirty-two years with the MTDC.

Summing Up

The fiscal year ending June 30, 2001, was marked by the achievement of an aggressive investment plan. Ten new companies were added to the portfolio:

- Analine Technologies, Inc., of Boston
- Brock Rogers Surgical, Inc., of Norwood
- CASTion Corporation of Ludlow
- Cognistar Corporation of Southborough
- Continuum Control Corporation of Billerica
- Geovue, Inc., of Boston
- Global Communication Devices, Inc., of North Andover
- Market Perspectives, Inc., of Framingham
- TerraTherm, Inc., of Fitchburg
- ThreeCore, Inc., of Danvers.

Follow-on investments in portfolio companies from the traditional investment fund were made. Seven new Commonwealth Fund investments were made in the following:

- Cardiofocus Inc. of Norton
- Clarity Imaging Technologies, Inc., of Springfield
- Connigstar Corporation of Southborough
- Geovue, Inc., of Boston
- Global Communication Devices, Inc., of North Andover
- Sprockets.com, Inc., of Boston
- Visionscope, Inc., of Ashland

As of January 2014, only TerraTherm and CASTion (now ThermoEnergy Corporation) from FY01 remained in the MTDC portfolio, along with Impress Systems, an FY00 investment. While the typical duration of a company in the portfolio was about seven years, these three firms were approaching the eighteen-year record set by Fotec.

Cumulative investments as of June 30, 2001, from the first investments of the traditional fund in 1980, totaled $56.9 million, and cumulative realized net gains were $34.2 million. As of December 2000, there were 11,100 people employed among the sixty-nine active companies that the MTDC had helped to finance. The annual payroll from these jobs was estimated to be $622 million, yielding annual payroll-related taxes of $194 million to the federal government and $30.6 million to the Commonwealth.

The Commonwealth Fund II program was closed with commitment of $12 million from the MTDC, $2 million from BancBoston Investments, Inc., and $1 million from the Essex Regional Retirement Board.

The market value of the portfolio as of June 30, 2001, was $24.6 million, and there was about $8 million in cash or equivalents in the treasury.

The MTDC board of directors included Paul Severino (chairman), Drew Hannah, Joseph Iandiorio (treasurer), Frank Manning (vice chairman), Alan Morse, Lita Nelsen (secretary), and Elizabeth Powell. In addition were the following ex officio members: the director of economic development, the secretary of administration and finance, and the president of the University of Massachusetts. Among the designees of the ex officio members, David Sheehan, Joseph Donovan, and David Lewis were consistent contributors over several years.

The investment staff members included Bob Crowley, Karin Gregory, Dina (Gordon) Routhier, Kevin Nixon, Suzanne Smetana, and Paul Tu. Gail Cormier and Mary Stack, longtime support staff members, joined them. These individuals were responsible for the day-to-day operations of the MTDC.

In particular, Bob Crowley, as executive vice president, served as the chief investment officer, staff training director and coach, and my partner in this endeavor for seventeen years. Gail Cormier, as executive assistant and office operations manager, was the institutional historian, principal liaison with the board, "Blue Book" preparation manager, and overall key team member from 1980 to today, where she still keeps the wheels turning.

I am tremendously proud of the accomplishments of the staff of the MTDC and the contributions made by the members of the board.

Conclusion

The 1980s and 1990s were exciting years to be engaged in helping to start and grow innovative technology-based companies. We were players in and witnesses to the building of the information-technology infrastructure, the emergence of computer software as a product independent from hardware, the early use of networked systems, and the rapid expansion of the Internet. We saw technologies deployed to solve problems in health care, environment monitoring and cleanup, factory automation, business communication, and so many other areas of daily life that we now take for granted. We had the pleasure to work with so many creative and resilient entrepreneurs, who devoted their lives to making their dreams become realities.

During those decades the venture capital investment world began to shift. In the 1980s in Massachusetts, venture capital consisted of a small group of highly collegial individuals from firms that were fully engaged in building new enterprises. There were individual investors, but angel investor groups were rare. By the end of the 1990s, venture capital and private equity firms emerged as an "industry" that not only backed start-ups, but also invested in existing companies, fueling growth before an IPO, and engaged in leveraged buyouts of large corporations. The amount of money under management by these firms grew into the billions, and thousands of new people entered what was becoming characterized as a "profession." The seed and early-stage venture investing community began to include several well-organized and well-recognized angel investor groups that took over the role of starting and building new companies.

MTDC was an experiment in 1978. There were ideologues who resisted the idea of the government setting up a venture capital fund. There were venture investors who feared that the government would be a competitor. There were skeptics who felt that no state agency could ever be run successfully as an investment firm. There were political partisans who did not want to see their opponents achieve success by introducing innovations.

By the beginning of the new millennium, the MTDC was viewed as a success. It had survived being stillborn when the charter was approved but no investment funds were appropriated. It had leveraged federal funds to begin making investments and gaining experience. It had developed a proven investment process that withstood potential political interference. It had developed a collaborative relationship with private venture investors. It had created a new vehicle for raising investment capital. It had identified and backed entrepreneurs who did accomplish their dreams. It had helped to create thousands of jobs. And it had become financially successful.

The new millennium would see big changes in both the technology sector and the venture capital industry. The foundations laid for the information-technology infrastructure, first with hardware and peripherals in the 1980s, and then with software and networking in the 1990s, now provided a robust platform for new ways to use computer technology in daily life. In a few years, the growth of wireless mobile technology would expand these uses to touch hundreds of millions of people around the world. Thousands of new ventures would be launched to address a wide array of market niches. In addition, new and growing life-science companies would create a seemingly insatiable demand for capital.

Venture capital firms would not only grow into large institutions, but many would shift their focus to private equity investments in established companies. Furthermore, regulatory changes in response to financial excesses would make it less feasible for small emerging companies to raise capital through initial public offerings.

There would be both opportunities and challenges for the MTDC as it continued its economic-development mission in this new environment.

CHAPTER 10

EPILOGUE

In 2012 the MTDC announced that it would be publicly known as MassVentures. An excerpt from the press release follows.

> **BOSTON, MA**, June 14, 2012—MTDC, the venture capital arm of the Commonwealth of Massachusetts, announced today that it is now operating under a new name, MassVentures, to support the formation and fuel the growth of innovative technology-driven companies in Massachusetts. This new name reflects new capital received to help identify and support promising entrepreneurs developing high-growth, technology-driven companies.
>
> Through **MassDevelopment's Emerging Technology Fund**, MassVentures will manage a new $5 million traditional investment capital fund to fill capital gaps (1) in emerging market segments not adequately served by the venture community, (2) of first-time entrepreneurs, and (3) with companies transitioning from seed to Series A funding. MassVentures expects to invest in four to seven new companies each year.

> In addition, MassVentures recently launched a $6 million SBIR targeted technologies (START) program that provides supplemental grant funding to qualified companies with SBIR Phase II funding to accelerate the commercialization and growth of promising technologies.[71]

The infusion of new capital into the investment fund had actually started a few years before, when in 2004 and 2006, the legislature appropriated $5 million and $2 million, respectively, as part of two different economic-stimulus bills. These represented the first new appropriations since 1988. What may have happened to change the attitude of the state government about using the MTDC as one of its instruments of economic development is an interesting story.

Need for More Ammunition

After the MTDC invested a record $11.9 million in FY01, the $4.8 million closed in FY02 consumed most of the extraordinary harvests of over $15 million from gains realized in FY00 and FY01. During the next two years, FY03 and FY04, the MTDC invested $692,673 and $577, 417, respectively. The dollars invested in these years represented the lowest levels of investment made by the corporation since 1986.

The Massachusetts economy was suffering in the early 2000s, especially in the technology sector. Once again political leadership to stimulate the economy was needed. In 2001, Governor Paul Cellucci resigned to become the ambassador to Canada and Lt. Governor Jane Swift became the acting governor. The following year, 2002, there would be an election of a new governor, Mitt Romney.

During these years of leadership transition, the Democrat-dominated legislature began to become more active in launching initiatives to spur economic development. In particular, the Speakers of the House of Representatives, Thomas Finneran and Salvatore DiMasi, and the Senate presidents, Thomas Birmingham and Robert Travaglini, were willing to support legislation based on jobs-creation ideas generated from within the legislature.

Once Governor Romney took office in 2003, he was faced with a $3 billion budget deficit. His priorities were to reduce taxes and streamline government operations. However, he also imposed fee increases that were designed to help fill the deficit gap. His approach to economic development included tax credits and reductions that would try to motivate business investments.

In addition to a political philosophy that was very different from the Democratic legislature, Governor Romney provided aggressive support for a campaign to elect more Republican legislators. When this did not result in success, the Democratic leadership seemed more emboldened.

The role of the MTDC did not fit with Governor Romney's political philosophy. While its charter required the MTDC to seek private sector coinvestors in its deals and it had leveraged more than $4 dollars of private funds for every public dollar invested, Governor Romney seemed to view the MTDC's role as a competitor of private venture capital firms. He vetoed the section of the economic-stimulus bill, Chapter 141 of the Acts of 2003, that included a $5 million appropriation for the MTDC investment fund. The legislature overrode the governor's veto. A few years later, the legislature approved an additional $2.5 million appropriation for the MTDC in Chapter 123 of the Acts of 2006.

While these infusions of cash would enable the corporation to help start new companies and create jobs, they did not address the fundamental need to have a predictable systematic way to raise new investment capital. Furthermore, the MTDC could not rely mainly on successful harvests from previous investments, as it did in the past. As mentioned above, the fact that the types of companies in which the MTDC invested could not exit through IPOs reduced the potential gains that could be realized from this source.

Governance Change

The election of a Democratic governor, Deval Patrick, in 2006 would change the political philosophy about the role of government in economic development. However, it would not be until his second term in 2012 that his administration would take an active role in securing new investment capital for the MTDC.

Before this would happen, his administration initiated a major reform of the governance and operations of the Massachusetts quasi-public organizations.[72] Chapter 240 of the Acts of 2010 provided that the chairman of each of the quasi-public corporations would be the secretary of housing and economic development. In the MTDC case, this would mean that the long history of having a private-sector person appointed by the governor would end and that an appointed public official would now lead the board.

Within a year of this governance change, the heads of several of the economic-development quasi-public entities were forced to resign or retire. In the case of the MTDC, Bob Crowley was encouraged to retire as president in 2011. Jerry Bird, who had been vice president of the MTDC, then replaced Bob as president. Fortunately, this leadership transition went smoothly, and the policies and investment process that had been critical to the MTDC's historic success were continued. It will be interesting to see what will happen in future years when there is a change in the governor. The first instance to observe this will be in 2015, when Governor Patrick leaves office and Republican Governor Charlie Baker takes his place.

Key Outcomes

Between FY02 and FY14, thirty new companies were added to the MassVentures portfolio. Total investments over this period were about $23.7 million. This brought the total number of companies in which MassVentures invested from its inception in 1978 to 139. As of the end of FY14, 118 of these companies had exited the portfolio.

Over the corporation's history through June 30, 2014, positive financial results had come from seventeen of the companies that had IPOs, twenty-eight that had been acquired or merged, and seven that had bought back their stock. Losses were realized from twenty-eight companies that were merged or acquired and thirty-seven that ceased operations. Total realized gains were $65.1 million and losses were $36.4 million, yielding net realized gains of $28.7 million. All of this was accomplished by investing a total of $15.7 million of public funds, $3 million from the federal government and $12.7 million from the Commonwealth.

The annual average number of jobs among active firms backed by MassVentures between 1984 and 2014 was about 5,400. Over this period, total payroll-related taxes were about $3 billion to the federal government and $438 million to the Commonwealth. In addition, there were many more indirect jobs among the local suppliers to these companies.

MassVentures Portfolio

As of January 2015, the companies in the MassVentures active portfolio that had received initial investments before FY02 included the following. The fiscal year in which the initial investment was closed and the industry sector for each company are detailed below:

- Courion (FY98) (security)
- Impress Systems (FY00) (industrial automation and robotics)
- Polatis (FY01) (systems and software)
- TerraTherm (FY01) (environmental technology)
- ThermoEnergy (FY01) (environmental technology)

These companies with more than ten years duration in the portfolio underscore MassVentures's ability to be a patient investor.

Companies added to the portfolio between June 2002 and January 2015 include:

- Tomophase (FY06) (medical devices)
- Owner IQ (FY08) (Internet and digital media)
- Applause (formerly UTest) (FY08) (systems and software)
- Ntirety (FY09) (systems and software)
- Forerun (FY09) (health-care IT)
- Life Image (FY09) (health-care IT)
- Harvest Automation (FY10) (industrial automation and robotics)
- Illume (FY11) (mobile)
- Vsnap.com (FY12) (Internet and digital media)
- Ubiqi Health (FY13) (health-care IT)
- Raven (FY13) (security)
- Curoverse (FY14) (health-care IT)
- Inside Tracker (FY14) (Internet and digital media)

These companies reflect the diverse types of technology-based enterprises that are spawned in Massachusetts. They were built upon foundations laid by the computer hardware and peripheral, software, and networking companies that were financed in the 1980s and 1990s. Several of these companies are poised for successful exits in the next few years and will provide additional capital for MassVentures to continue its mission.

Venture Capital in 2013/2014

On January 17, 2014, the PWC Money Tree issued a press release that reported:

> Venture capitalists invested $29.4 billion in 3,995 deals in 2013, an increase of 7 percent in dollars and a 4 percent increase in deals over the prior year, according to the MoneyTree Report by PricewaterhouseCoopers LLP and the National Venture Capital Association (NVCA), based on data from Thomson Reuters. In Q4 2013 alone, $8.4 billion went into 1,077 deals.

The report also stated that

> Internet-specific companies captured $7.1 billion in 2013, marking the highest level of Internet investment since 2001. Additionally, annual investments into the Software industry also reached the highest level since 2000 with $11.0 billion flowing into 1,523 deals in 2013.[73]

The press release indicated that in 2013, the average investment in all companies was $7.4 million, while for Internet deals it was $6.7 million, the same as in 2012. All seed-stage deals averaged $4.3 million in 2013. This was an increase from $2.8 million in 2012. These numbers underscored that the capital gap for very early-stage technology companies had widened once again.

According to a *Boston Globe* article also published on January 17, 2014, based on the PWC Money Tree Report, Silicon Valley companies captured $12.1 billion, 41 percent of the total in 2013.[74] New England firms received $3.3 billion, 11 percent of the total, with New York companies close behind with $3.2 billion. In New England, biotechnology companies received the largest amount, $978.5 million.

Software companies were second, with $793 million. The average deal size for biotechnology companies was $11 million, and for software companies it was $6.2 million.

Most of the New England venture capital–backed companies are located in Massachusetts. It is quite reasonable to assume that these deals are comparable in average deal size to those nationally. With seed-stage deals averaging $4.3 million, major venture capital firms are backing companies that do not have the typical profile of those in MassVentures's target market.

Angel investor groups have helped to fill the financing gap for seed and early-stage start-ups. More recently, crowdfunding sources have been used to help launch new enterprises. However, these types of investors generally do not have deep financial pockets to enable their companies to withstand severe financial downturns or to support very rapid growth.

Future Opportunities

While the amount of venture capital available for Massachusetts firms is at another cyclical high, there is still a capital gap faced by small technology-based start-ups. MassVentures conducted a survey in 2013, the results of which indicated that companies trying to raise $1 to $3 million from professional venture capital investors were continuing to have difficulty. This was especially the case if the founders are first-time entrepreneurs and the markets for their innovative application of technology are not yet developed. This capital gap has been chronic over the past thirty-five years, and there is no indication that it will go away in the future.

Massachusetts is fortunate to have universities, research centers, and technology companies that nurture new generations of technology-oriented entrepreneurs. These men and women are the critical resource for the Massachusetts innovation economy. MassVentures provides a supportive role in helping these entrepreneurs sharpen their business plans and find ways to finance their enterprises.

Public-Private Partnership

Much has been written about the success and failures of public-private partnerships. MassVentures is one of the great success stories. From what was an experiment in 1978, we have learned lessons of how to maintain this success. Political leaders can look to MassVentures to understand both the opportunities and challenges in using venture capital to support economic development in the future. The question is whether these leaders will choose to employ practical solutions to problems or become frozen by political ideology. My hunch is that they will follow the path that the Commonwealth has blazed since the seventeenth century and leverage private profit objectives with public investments.

ENDNOTES

Introduction

1 "An Economic Program for Massachusetts," by Governor Dukakis Administration, August 1976, p. 16.

Chapter 1: Beginnings

2 "A Brief History of the Pilgrims by Ron Collins," www.mayflowerfamilies.com/?page_id=194.

3 "History," www.newenglandcouncil.com/about/history/.

4 *Creative Capital: George Doriot and the Birth of Venture Capital*, by Spencer E. Ante (Boston: Harvard Business Press, 2008), pp. 107–110.

5 Massachusetts General Laws, Chapter 843, Acts of 1969, created the Massachusetts Science and Technology Foundation.

6 "A Proposal for Funding Support to Establish the Massachusetts Technology Development Corporation," by Dr. John Silvers, Director of the Massachusetts Science and Technology Foundation, August 1975, 1–2.

7 MTDC Enabling Act, Chapter 497, Acts of 1978, amending Chapter 40G of the Massachusetts General Laws.

8 "New Group Puts Its Cash Where There Isn't Any," by David Warsh, *Boston Globe,* June 6, 1979, an editorial regarding the establishment of the MTDC.

9 "Technology Entrepreneurship: Analyses from the MTDC Portfolio," Individual Leadership Project by Rob Frohman for MS in Engineering Management at the Tufts Gordon Institute, August 2012, p. 17. This was a series of interviews with former MTDC entrepreneurs.

10 Ibid.

Chapter 2: Growing the Corporation

11 See "The IBM Tramp," by Stephen Papson, *Jump Cut: A Review of Contemporary Media, 1990, 2006: History of the Introduction of the IBM PC,* no. 35, April 1990, pp. 66–72.

12 "Technology Entrepreneurship: Analyses from the MTDC Portfolio," Individual Leadership Project by Rob Frohman for MS in Engineering Management at the Tufts Gordon Institute, August 2012, p. 11. This was a series of interviews with former MTDC entrepreneurs..

13 Ibid, p. 14.

14 Ibid, pp. 15–16.

15 "Economic Innovation International, Inc.," www.economic-innovation.com/about_us.htm, description of Economic Innovation consulting firm headed by Belden Daniels.

16 E-mail from Belden Daniels to John Hodgman, June 27, 2014.

Chapter 3: Becoming Self-Sustaining

17 "Creating the Future," by Governor Dukakis Administration, spring 1987.

18 *Wall Street Journal,* by Staff, March 1987, page not available.

19 MTDC FY87 Annual Report, p. 12, footnote 1.

20 MTDC FY88 Annual Report, p. 14, footnote 1.

21 "The Duke: Miracle or Mirage," by Ann Reilly Dowd, *Fortune Magazine,* May 23, 1988, pp. 102–104.

22 "The Real Estate Cycle and the Economy: Consequences of the Massachusetts Boom of 1984–87," a report by Karl E. Case to the Boston

Federal Reserve Bank. Available at http://www.bos.frb.org/economic/neer/neer1991/neer591c.pdf.

Chapter 4: Negotiating a New Role

23 "Winning in the Nineties: An Economic Strategy for Massachusetts," by Governor Dukakis Administration, January 1990.

24 "Bank of New England Corporation," Chapter 8 of Part II of *Managing the Crisis: The FDIC and RTC Experience,* by the Federal Deposit Insurance Corporation (1998), gives the history of the takeover of the Bank of New England. It is available at http://www.fdic.gov/bank/historical/managing/history2-08.pdf.

25 "For Start-ups, Funding Squeeze Tightens," by Udayan Gupta, *Wall Street Journal,* December 28, 1989, Enterprise Section.

26 Massachusetts General Laws, Chapter 40G, Section 3: MTDC enabling act.

27 Ibid.

28 MTDC, Board of Directors Minutes, February 27, 1991.

Chapter 5: Venture Investing Challenges

29 "Venture Capital Disbursements Declined 43% to $2 Billion in 1990," by John G. Bonnanzio, *Venture Capital Journal*, June 1991, pp. 14–19.

30 *SBA News,* May 2, 1991, page not available.

31 "An Advisory Committee on the Coordination of the Economic Development Programs of the Commonwealth," Governor's Executive Order, January 17, 1993.

32 "Long Dismissed by Venture Capitalists, State Programs Are Gaining Respect," by John Bonnanzio, *Venture Capital Journal*, August 1991, p. 24.

33 Ibid, p. 27.

34 US House Committee on Science, Space, and Technology, January 1, 1993, report by the Committee regarding the proposed legislation.

35 "Technology Entrepreneurship: Analyses from the MTDC Portfolio," Individual Leadership Project by Rob Frohman for MS in Engineering Management at the Tufts Gordon Institute, August 2012, pp. 13–14. This was a series of interviews with former MTDC entrepreneurs.

36 Ibid, p. 15.

37 Ibid, pp. 12–13.

38 E-mail from Tom Ricciardelli to John Hodgman, March 2014.

Chapter 6: Before the Internet

39 Series of three articles on the MTDC, by Patrick Porter, *Mass High Tech*: "State's Venture Firm Breeds Winners: This Small But Innovative Government Agency Has Paid Big Dividends," February 22–March 7, 1993; "MTDC Manages Patient and Brave Money: Entrepreneur and Venture Pros Give the Quasi-Public Agency High Marks," March 8–21; "Entrepreneurs Turn to MTDC for Early Stage Money: Hodgman and Crowley Make Profits and Create Jobs by Investing in the State's Startup Companies," March 22–April 4, 1993; pages not available.

40 *Boston Globe,* by Staff, March 28, 1993, page not available.

41 "A Company Founder Who Bet His Ranch," by Glen Rifkin, *New York Times Sunday Magazine*, April 4, 1993.

42 *Boston Globe,* by Staff, March 9, 1994, page not available.

43 "Looser Times at Start-up High: Early-Stage Investing Faucet Back On after Early 1990s Shut Off," by Mario Shao, *Boston Globe*, March 9, 1994, page not available.

44 "Dream Team Examines State's VC Needs," by Staff, *Boston Business Journal*, March 10–16, 1995, page not available.

45 "*Boston Globe*/Price Waterhouse Survey of Venture Capital Investments, 3rd and 4th Quarters 1995," by Staff, *Boston Globe*, December 10, 1995, page not available; and February 25, 1996, p. 72.

46 "List of 3rd Quarter 1995 Initial Public Offerings," by Staff, *Boston Globe*, December 10, 1995, page not available.

47 "The Funding Gap for Smaller Funds," by Richard Testa, *Testa, Hurwitz, and Thibault Newsletter*, Winter 1996, page not available.

48 "VC Fund Raising Hit New High in 1995," by Renee Deger, *Venture Capital Journal*, February 1996, pp. 36–39.

49 "Seed Fund Alliance Shelved," by Staff, *Private Equity Analyst,* April 1997, page not available.

Chapter 7: Waltzing with the Elephants

50 "List of Largest Venture Capital Firms in Boston," compiled by Erin Duffy, *Boston Business Journal,* March 1996, page not available.

51 "Report of Price Waterhouse Survey of Venture Capital Investments for the Last Quarter 1995," by Staff, *Boston Globe*, February 25, 1996, p. 72; and Price Waterhouse Survey of Venture Capital Investments, June 1996.

52 "Second Quarter Shatters Record for VC Funding," by Todd Hyten, *Boston Business Journal,* August 9–15, 1996, page not available.

53 "Report of Massachusetts Companies Receiving Venture Capital Investment in the 3rd Quarter of 1996," by Staff, *Boston Business Journal*, November 1996, page not available.

54 "*Boston Globe*/Price Waterhouse Survey of Venture Capital Investments for the 4th Quarter 1996," by Staff, *Boston Globe*, February 28, 1997, page not available.

55 "List of 4th Quarter 1996 Initial Public Offerings," by Staff, *Boston Globe*, February 28, 1997, page not available.

56 "Technology Entrepreneurship: Analyses from the MTDC Portfolio," Individual Leadership Project by Rob Frohman for MS in Engineering Management at the Tufts Gordon Institute, August 2012, p. 12. This was a series of interviews with former MTDC entrepreneurs.

57 Ibid, pp. 16–17.

58 "The First Venture Capital Fund Ever Developed in Western Massachusetts," Report by Tom Chmura, Vice President for Economic Development of the University of Massachusetts, February 1997.

59 "Report of the Closing of $13 Million for the MASS Ventures Equity Fund, by Staff, *Boston Business Journal*, March 21–27, 1997, page not available.

Chapter 8: Evolving the Model

[60] Letter from John Hodgman to the Chairman of the House Committee on Science and Technology, Representative Lida Harkins, May 12, 1997.

[61] *Boston Globe* Venture/PWC Money Tree Reports for Quarters 3 and 4 of 1997 and Four Quarters of 1998, by Staff, *Boston Globe*, December 1997; February 2, 1998; May 17, 1998; September 2, 1998; November 15, 1998; and May 16, 1999, pages not available.

Chapter 9: The Internet Era Arrives

[62] Historical trend data from PricewaterhouseCoopers National Venture Capital Association, available at https://www.pwcmoneytree.com/HistoricTrends/CustomQueryHistoricTrend.

[63] "Two Golden Words: Internet Related," by Jerry Ackerman, *Boston Globe*, February 14, 1999, p. F1.

[64] "VCs Rake in $22 B in 1998," by Staff, *Venture Capital Journal*, February 1999, pp. 5 and 18.

[65] "Too Venturesome? Fast Pace of Financing Deals Has Some Investors Worried," by Ron Rosenberg, *Boston Globe*, August 18, 1999, p. F4.

[66] *Boston Globe*/PWC Money Tree Venture Capital Reports for 2000, by Staff, *Boston Globe*, May 14, 2000; August 13, 2000; November 12, 2000; and February 16, 2001, pages not available.

[67] Zweig Letter 2013 Hot Firm List, August 2013, available at https://zweiggroup.com/conference/hotfirm/2013hotfirm-list.php.

[68] Price Waterhouse Coopers Money Tree Report Third Quarter 2000, December 2000, by Staff, page not available.

[69] "DeNucci Questions Proposed Financial Bonuses for Two Officers of Tech Corp," State Auditor Press Release, January 25, 2001.

[70] "Massachusetts—Economy," City-Data.com, available at http://www.city-data.com/states/Massachusetts-Economy.html.

Chapter 10: Epilogue

71 MTDC press release, June 14, 2012, available at http://mass-ventures.com/in-the-news-2/in-the-news-2/.

72 Massachusetts General Laws, Chapter 240 Acts of 2010.

73 PWC Money Tree press release, January 17, 2014, available at http://www.pwc.com/us/en/press-releases/2014/annual-venture-investment-dollars.jhtml.

74 PWC Money Tree Report, by Staff, *Boston Globe*, January 17, 2014, page not available.

APPENDIX

The board of directors and officers of the MTDC were critical to its success. Below is a list of these individuals with whom I served during my tenure as president from 1984 to 2001.

The members of the board of directors and officers in FY83, the year before I joined the corporation, included the following:

- Howard N. Smith, chairman: president of Kurzweil Computer Products, Inc.
- Orie L. Dudley Jr.: president of the Omega Fund, Endowment Management Research Corporation
- Dr. John R. Ehrenfeld: senior consultant, Arthur D. Little, Inc.
- Joseph S. Iandiorio, Esquire: patent counsel
- Dr. Judith H. Obermayer: president, Obermayer Associates
- Dr. Robert C. Seamans Jr.: Henry Luce Professor of Public Policy, MIT
- Arthur M. Vash: corporate director

Ex officio members were:

- Frank T. Keefe: secretary of administration and finance
- John F. Kerry: lieutenant governor
- Evelyn F. Murphy: secretary of economic affairs
- William F. Aikman: president and CEO of the MTDC

In FY84, Orie Dudley and Arthur Vash stepped down from the board, and the following new members were appointed by Governor Dukakis:

- Timothy J. McNeill: vice president, corporate development, International Data Group, Inc.
- Phyllis Sherry Swersky: senior vice president, finance, Cullinet Software, Inc.

The board of directors elected the following officers:

- President and CEO of the MTDC: John F. Hodgman
- Vice president of the MTDC: Robert J. Crowley

In FY85, Dr. Robert Seamans stepped down from the board, and Governor Dukakis appointed:

- Ron E. Payne: corporate purchasing manager, Digital Equipment Corporation
- Professor David N. Wormley: head, Engineering Department, MIT

Ex officio member:

- Dr. Alden S. Raine: director, Governor's Office of Economic Development

In FY86, Governor Dukakis appointed:

Ex officio member:

- Joseph Alviani: secretary of economic affairs

There were no changes in FY87.

In FY88, John Ehrenfeld and Judith Obermayer stepped down, and Governor Dukakis appointed:

- Horace W. Furumoto: president of Candela Laser Corporation
- Mary Makela: president of Cognos Corporation

In FY89, Secretary Alviani stepped down, and Governor Dukakis appointed Alden Raine as secretary of economic affairs and appointed:

Ex officio member:

- L. Edward Lashman Jr.: secretary of administration and finance

In FY90, Howard Smith stepped down, and Governor Dukakis appointed David Wormley as chairman and appointed:

- Benjamin Kincannon: consultant

In FY91 Governor Weld appointed:

- Andrew G. Mills: president, Thomson Financial Networks

Ex officio members:

- Daniel S. Gregory: secretary of economic affairs
- Peter Nessen: secretary of administration and finance
- R. Piedad Robertson: secretary of education

The board of directors elected the following officers:

- Executive vice president of the MTDC: Robert J. Crowley
- Vice president of the MTDC: Michael E. A. O'Malley

In FY92 Mary Makela, Timothy McNeill, David Wormley, and Secretary Daniel Gregory stepped down, and Governor Weld appointed:

- Michael Crossen, Esquire: Rubin & Rudman
- Paul Severino: president of Wellfeet Communications, Inc.

Ex officio member:

- Stephen Tocco: secretary of economic affairs

In FY93 Secretary Peter Nessen and Secretary Stephen Tocco stepped down, and Governor Weld appointed Andrew Mills as chairman and appointed:

Ex officio members:

- Gloria Larson: secretary of economic affairs
- Mark Robinson: secretary of administration and finance

In FY94 Horace Furumoto, Benjamin Kincannon, Phyllis Swersky, and Secretary Mark Robinson stepped down, and Governor Weld appointed:

- C. Christopher Alberti: managing director, Prager, McCarthy and Sealy
- Lita L. Nelson: director of the Technology Licensing Office, MIT
- Elizabeth P. Powell: chairman of the board, Diamond Machining Technology, Inc.
- Bruce Stangle: chairman, Analysis Group, Inc.
- Dorothy A. Terrell: president, Sun Express, Inc.

Ex officio member:

- Charles D. Baker: secretary of administration and finance

In FY95 Secretary Piedad Robertson stepped down.

Michael O'Malley resigned from the MTDC, and Robert J. Creeden was elected vice president.

In FY96, Andrew Mills stepped down as chairman, and Governor Weld appointed Paul Severino to replace him. Secretary Gloria Larson stepped down, and Governor Weld appointed:

Ex officio member:

- David A. Tibbetts: director, department of economic development

In FY97, Andrew Mills stepped down, and Governor Weld appointed:

Ex officio member:

- William Bulger: president, University of Massachusetts

In FY98 Christopher Alberti and Secretary Baker stepped down, and Governor Cellucci appointed:

- Frank B. Manning: president, Zoom Telephonics, Inc.
- Alan R. Morse Jr.: chairman of the board, Harvard Pilgrim Health Care

Ex officio member:

- Frederick Laskey: secretary of administration and finance

In FY99, David Tibbetts and Frederick Laskey stepped down, and Governor Cellucci appointed:

Ex officio members:

- Carol Boviard: director, department of economic development
- Andrew Natsios: secretary of administration and finance

Robert Creeden, vice president of the MTDC, resigned.

In FY00 Dorothy Terrell, Carol Boviard, and Andrew Natsios stepped down, and Governor Cellucci appointed:

- Drew Hannah: CEO, Parker Guitars and Fishman Transducers, Inc.

Ex officio members:

- Elizabeth Ames: director, department of economic development
- Stephen Crosby: secretary of economic development

The board of directors elected Karin A. Gregory vice president of the MTDC.

In addition to the list above, I have described some of the key changes in board members and staff over my tenure with the corporation.

Changes in Board Leadership in 1990

Before leaving office at the end of 1990, Governor Dukakis accepted the resignation of Howard Smith as chairman of the board and appointed David Wormley a sitting board member. At that time, Dr. Wormley was the head of the mechanical engineering department at MIT.

By April 1991, Howard Smith had resigned from the board and retired to live in Williamstown, Massachusetts. This brought to an end his involvement in creating the MTDC in 1978 and his stewardship of the corporation since 1983. Howard had been a formidable board member, especially regarding the many investment decisions that were made during those years. He had also been my boss since 1984. Howard's approach as a no-nonsense, problem-solving businessman and public official had often set the tone of the board meetings.

David Wormley brought a different style of leadership. He was a very thoughtful and considerate person who had a distinguished career in academia. His approach was collaborative and deliberate, taking into consideration the views of all the board members.

Dan Daly's role as the representative of the secretary of economic affairs was also very important. He brought the perspective and priorities of the new administration to the table. He also had business experience as an executive-search professional who had helped many technology companies find key talent. Later, this expertise became very helpful when we needed to recruit new board members.

In July 1991, Andy Mills joined the board as the first former portfolio company executive to be appointed by the governor. He had headed Business Research Corporation, which was subsequently acquired by Thomson International. Andy was then tapped to be the president of the new entity, which was headquartered in Boston. This company grew to employ several thousand people in the region. The governor ultimately appointed Andy chairman of the MTDC board in 1993.

Changes in Board Leadership and Staff 1993–1994

By 1993, Governor Weld had appointed three new private-sector members to the board of directors: Andy Mills, Paul Severino, and Michael Crossen. Andy Mills had been elected vice chairman by the board and acted as chair when David Wormley left MIT to become dean of the school of engineering at Penn State. The governor later appointed Andy chairman of the board. Paul Severino was a successful entrepreneur, who at the time of his appointment was CEO and founder of Wellfleet Communications, Inc. He was elected by the board to serve as secretary. Michael Crossen was an attorney with the firm of Rubin and Rudman.

During the previous year, Governor Weld had appointed several new board members. They included Christopher Alberti, an investment banker; Dorothy Terrell, a technology-company executive; and Elizabeth Powell, a cofounder of a small business. In addition, Bob Crowley was elected executive vice president, and Mike O'Malley was elected vice president. Bob Creeden and a new investment analyst, Will Wilcoxson, completed the complement of investment staff.

By the end of FY94, Michael Crossen had resigned from the board and the governor had appointed three new members: Lita Nelsen, Bruce Stangle, and Dorothy Terrell. Lita Nelsen was the director of the technology licensing office at MIT. Her appointment continued the tradition going back to the founding of the MTDC of having a representative of MIT on its board. Bruce Stangle was a cofounder of the Analysis Group Inc. Dorothy was president of Sun Express, Inc.

Together with Andy Mills, chairman of the MTDC board; Paul Severino, vice chairman (later chairman in 1996); and Joseph Iandiorio, treasurer, these eight individuals would lead the governance of the corporation and the focus of the investment program for the next few years.

In 1998, after Chris Alberti and Andy Mills resigned from the board, Governor Cellucci appointed Frank Manning, president of Zoom Telephonics, Inc., a former portfolio-company CEO, and Alan Morse, chairman of Harvard Pilgrim Health Care.

Between 1994 and 1998, the MTDC also benefited from the support of the designees of the three ex officio members of the board: the secretary of administration and finance, the secretary of economic affairs, and the secretary of education (later the president of the University of Massachusetts). They were an impressive and dedicated group who would help to guide the future of the MTDC in the 1990s.

Staff Changes 1995–1999

In the spring of 1995, Mike O'Malley accepted a position with the venture capital group of the Memorial Drive Trust. He joined the alumni of the MTDC who had gone on to continue successful careers with private-sector venture capital firms.

By June 1995 Bob Creeden was elected to be vice president of the MTDC. Will Wilcoxson had become an experienced associate. Kathleen Birmingham and Mark Grader joined the corporation as new investment staff members.

During FY99, Bob Creeden and Will Wilcoxson decided to accept positions with two different private venture capital firms. These jobs provided opportunities for Bob and Will to exercise their skill and knowledge while earning significantly more compensation. Unfortunately, the gain-share plan that was implemented earlier that year was not sufficient to prevent these losses.

Once again we had to recruit and train new investment staff members. Bob Crowley would be especially critical as the person who would oversee and mentor the new team members. By the summer of 1999, Karin Gregory had been promoted to senior associate, Julie Lewis had a year of experience as an associate, and Paul Tu had joined the corporation as a new associate. In the fall, Dina Gordon would be added as a new associate. Karin would later be elected vice president in FY00.

Throughout my seventeen years with the corporation, Bob Crowley, executive vice president, was my partner. His dedication and experience were invaluable. In addition, longtime members of the support staff—Karen Butts, Esther Larson, Gail Cormier, Marie Phaneuf, and Mary Stack—completed the team.

SELECTED BIBLIOGRAPHY

In addition to the sources directly cited in the notes, in the writing of this book I relied greatly on my own personal collection of papers from 1984 to 2001, including

- Internal Reports, Memoranda, and Notes;
- MTDC Board of Directors' Agendas and Meeting Minutes; and
- MTDC Annual Reports from 1983 to 2013.

INDEX

C

D

E

F

G

H

I

J

K

L

M

N

O

P

Q

V

W

X

Y

Z

Printed in the United States
By Bookmasters